The
Presidential
Appointee's Handbook

The
Presidential
Appointee's Handbook

G. Edward DeSeve

BROOKINGS INSTITUTION PRESS
Washington, D.C.

Copyright © 2009
BROOKINGS INSTITUTION PRESS
1775 Massachusetts Avenue, N.W., Washington, D.C. 20036
www.brookings.edu

Library of Congress Cataloging-in-Publication data

DeSeve, G. Edward.
  The presidential appointee's handbook / G. Edward DeSeve.
    p.   cm.
  Includes bibliographical references and index.
  Summary: "Explains the core competencies that distinguish successful presidential appointees. Draws on ideas developed by scholars of public and business management, as well as years of government service. Presents a guide to the key terms, laws, and regulations that new appointees will have to deal with once in office"—Provided by publisher.
  ISBN 978-0-8157-1833-8 (pbk. : alk. paper)
  1. United States—Officials and employees—Selection and appointment. 2. Cabinet officers—Selection and appointment—United States. 3. Government executives—Selection and appointment—United States. 4. Judges—Selection and appointment—United States. 5. Presidents—United States. I. Title.
  JK731.D47 2008
  352.3—dc22
                                             2008044209

9 8 7 6 5 4 3 2 1

The paper used in this publication meets minimum requirements of the American National Standard for Information Sciences—Permanence of Paper for Printed Library Materials: ANSI Z39.48-1992.

Typeset in Sabon and Ocean

Composition by Cynthia Stock
Silver Spring, Maryland

Printed by R. R. Donnelley
Harrisonburg, Virginia

Contents

Foreword

As a presidential appointee of former presidents Ronald Reagan, George H. W. Bush, and Bill Clinton and a past head of three federal agencies spanning both the executive and legislative branches of government, I can assure you that, as a new presidential appointee, you are embarking on one of the most challenging and fulfilling jobs you will ever have. This handbook is designed to help you get off to a faster start and to enhance your ability to make a difference by benefiting from lessons learned by others who have preceded you. I encourage you to do your homework and to heed the words here. After all, your time in government is limited and the challenges that we face as a nation are great. The American people need you to be successful in whatever role you undertake on their behalf.

First and foremost, as a presidential appointee you have been provided with an opportunity that few Americans will ever have. If you are in a position that requires Senate confirmation, you will have the right, should you so choose, to use the prefix The Honorable (or Hon.) for the balance of your days on this earth. There is a reason for this: public service is a high calling, and serving your country in a position of significant responsibility is an honor and a privilege.

You have been selected to be a presidential appointee because the president has confidence in your ability and believes that your political philosophy is generally compatible with his. While in office, if you are in a policy-related position, you will generally be expected to contribute to and support whatever policies the president adopts. It you find that you are unable to do so, you should resign your position.

Your duty is not, however, only to the president. As a government official, you have a duty to the collective best interests of all Americans. In the final analysis, all presidential appointees work for the American people. So does the president and so do all civil servants. And, by the way, the civil servants with whom I worked were among the most highly educated, capable, and loyal individuals I have encountered throughout my thirty-five-plus years of work experience, more than twenty of them in the private sector. You should partner with senior executives in the civil service and draw on their experience, knowledge, and memory to help you achieve as much as possible during your necessarily limited tenure.

Leadership is especially challenging in government. Why? Because, compared to the private sector, in government you have many more players who think they are your boss, transparency is much greater, there are more rules and requirements and therefore less flexibility, and there is less continuity of leadership, primarily due to the limited tenure of political appointees. Moreover, you are more likely to encounter resistance to change.

Government employees have a tendency to be risk averse and process oriented, rather than results oriented. In order to lead effectively in this environment, you need to focus on achieving outcome-oriented results during your tenure. Since your time in office is limited, you should focus on a few goals, those that can either be achieved during your tenure or for which a significant milestone can be attained. You should make sure that all key players understand what these goals are and that key players' performances will be evaluated in part on their helping to achieve these goals. At the same time, however, keep in mind that process does matter, especially in connection with complex and controversial issues. In particular, the process you follow must involve adequate transparency and respect due process.

The importance of both outcomes and process may be reflected in your agency's values. Most world-class organizations, including the U.S. military services, operate on a set of core values. At the Government Accountability Office (GAO) we adopted the core values of accountability, integrity, and reliability. They served as positive beliefs and specific boundaries for all decisionmaking within the organization. I encourage you to consider adopting and communicating a set of such values if your agency does not already have them.

Partnering for progress with other federal agencies, with other levels of government, and with the private and not-for-profit sectors can help you maximize value and mitigate risk within current and available resource levels. Don't waste your time participating in turf wars even though some may want you to. In the end, it is results that count and those affected are not concerned with who delivers them.

I also recommend strongly that you make a regular practice of reaching outside your agency and outside Washington to keep in touch with the people you serve. As President Reagan said, "Washington is an island surrounded by a sea of reality." People in Washington, especially those in and around government, tend to be interested in power, policy, and politics. Most citizens throughout the rest of America have a different perspective, and many are skeptical of the federal government. It will serve you well to keep yourself abreast of opinion and issues in both worlds and to build bridges between them.

The press can also be a key ally in this task. The press can help you educate the public and set the record straight. You will learn over time which journalists you can trust and which ones you need to be more cautious with.

It is important to remember that the press is protected under our Constitution and has an important role to play in keeping the American people informed and holding government accountable. You may or may not like certain publications, networks, journalists, or commentators, but you should be evenhanded in dealing with all members of the media, including bloggers. I was fortunate in having good relations with the press during my time in government. This was due, in part, to making sure that our agency had a first-rate professional public affairs director and in part to my handling in a timely manner all legitimate press and media inquiries.

When dealing with the press, I always assumed that anything that I said was on the record unless there was an express understanding in advance to the contrary. In general, presidential appointees should comment only on the record. The only exception is when you provide background information to help reporters understand an issue before you go on the record to answer their questions.

Beyond the press, two other groups have more formal oversight roles. The first is Congress, which has a constitutional responsibility to oversee the executive branch. It conducts this responsibility through various committees—and with varying degrees of frequency and zeal. Your role is to give congressional members and staff the facts, to help them understand what you are doing and why, and to try to not take their criticisms personally.

The second more formal oversight group is the accountability community. This is composed primarily of various inspectors general and the GAO, the legislative branch agency that I headed from 1998 to 2008. Inspectors general have various investigative and audit responsibilities. The GAO has these as well as various evaluation, adjudicatory, and policy analysis responsibilities.

Accountability organizations are independent and will often provide some criticism, usually accurate and constructive, of executive branch operations. They can be very helpful to a presidential appointee who is trying to make much needed and long overdue changes. If such changes make sense, they can provide independent and authoritative validation and support.

As a presidential appointee, you must lead by example and practice what you preach. You must also demonstrate a strong commitment to the core values of your organization. You should demonstrate courage, integrity, vision, and stewardship. And don't forget, if you are trying to make tough and controversial changes, it will take time, along with patience, persistence, perseverance, and pain before you are likely to prevail.

Congratulations on your selection and good luck in your new responsibilities.

HON. DAVID M. WALKER
President and CEO, Peter G. Peterson Foundation
Former Comptroller General of the United States

Acknowledgments

This handbook is for you, the new or prospective presidential appointee. Copies are also intended for the members of the federal executive corps—senior executives, generals, admirals, and others—with whom you will serve. Having a strong presidential team to develop policy, advocate for programs, and create positive results requires that the roles and responsibilities of all members of the federal management team and others who work with it are clear to all parties.

This handbook is the product of many individuals and groups. In particular, I would like to thank Jonathan Breul, Gerry DeSeve, Charles Field, Chris Foreman, Steve Goldsmith, Mary Ellen Joyce, Don Kettl, Josh Koskinen, David Langlieb, Mike Mears, Chris Mihm, Alan Paller, Carol Pearson, Mac Reed, Alice Rivlin, Ron Sanders, Hannah Sistare, Stan Soloway, and Clifton Williams. At Brookings Institution Press, thanks go to Robert Faherty, Mary Kwak, and Susan Woollen, and to Diane Hammond for editing the manuscript. David Walker's foreword reflects his additional keen "insight, oversight, and foresight."

Special thanks to Grant Thornton LLP's Global Public Sector Practice for its generous support of the handbook. In particular, Morgan Kinghorn, chief operating officer, and Michael Hettinger, partner, supplied significant assistance.

In my own service in the federal government, I made friends and established relationships that have enriched my life for more than a decade. While your time in government may appear short, the intensity of your experience will make your service incredibly memorable. There will be high points and low points. However, your goal throughout your time in government should be to serve the president and the country to the best of your ability. All who contributed to this handbook hope and believe that the insights contained here can help you to provide that kind of service.

PART I

Competencies of a Presidential Appointee

The purpose of this handbook is to share with you as new presidential appointees the experiences of others who have held these appointments before you. The first part details six areas of competence that former presidential appointees have found to be essential for effective performance. The second part presents a set of documents that will constitute essential reference material throughout your tenure in office.

The six competencies addressed in this book are
—Leading for results
—Managing change and innovation
—Providing technical knowledge and ability
—Leading others
—Leading yourself
—Maintaining global awareness

Any list is arbitrary to some extent, and this one is no exception. Some analysts might include more competencies; others, fewer. For example, the Office of Personnel Management identifies five executive core qualifications as requirements for entry to the senior executive service: leading change, leading people, results driven, business acumen, and building coalitions. These core qualifications are further broken down into twenty-two subcompetencies, such as strategic thinking, team building, and financial, human capital, and technology management.[1]

The decision to focus on the six competencies listed above is based on both a careful review of various competency frameworks and conversations with many presidential appointees about the skills that were critical to their ability to do their jobs. While this framework does not include every aspect of competencies that all experts have identified, it highlights the most important behaviors that presidential appointees must master in order to perform effectively. Presidential appointees come to their office with strong backgrounds and skills. The competencies presented here provide a road map for the journey you are about to take. The road map will remind you of where you are going and may provide some good directions on how to get there.

Themes

Four major themes emerge from this handbook. These themes, as in music or art, recur and lend continuity to the work. They are
—Commitment and conflict
—Character, competence, and courage
—Continual learning
—Informed behavior

Commitment and Conflict

As a presidential appointee, you are here because you have answered a call to serve. Whatever your motivation, you are undertaking a commitment that will involve you in the most important questions facing the nation. In some cases, the policies and the direction of the administration will be fully consistent with your own views. At other times you will challenge these policies and test them against your own ideals and codes of behavior. In either case, you will need a firm commitment to engage in the honest work before you.

It will not always be easy to reconcile your personal ideals and views with those of the administration in which you serve. The history of government service by presidential appointees is replete with stories of these conflicts of conscience. Sometimes the only course is to resign. More often, you will seek to shape the policies in a way that seems most beneficial to the future of the nation as you see it. In any case, loyalty to the president must be weighed with loyalty to the country you serve and to your own convictions. You can be sure that in your administration, conflicts and commitments will clash in a public way. The media and critics of the administration are always looking to magnify honest differences of opinions into open hostilities. Your own behavior must be guided by your honest beliefs and by a code of conduct that embraces civility while not ignoring your conscience.

Character, Competence, and Courage

To answer the call to service and to have an informed commitment that enables you to deal with the challenges inherent in the conflicts you will face, you will need character, competence, and courage. Your character has been developed over your entire lifetime and will continue to be molded in your current assignment. While it is difficult to change the habits of a lifetime, it is possible to learn new elements of behavior—called *competencies* here—that are needed to respond to new challenges. A competency is "an underlying characteristic of a person in that it may be a motive, trait, skill, aspect of one's self-image or social role, or a body of knowledge which he or she uses."[2] This definition combines two aspects of competency—behaviors and skills—into a single set of characteristics. As the competency scholar Mary Ellen Joyce notes, "While competencies are meant to denote effective *behaviors,* many models include knowledge, expertise . . . and other managerial characteristics. There is a great need for the field to more clearly define and explain competency modeling."[3] This handbook uses the broader definition throughout. You already possess competency in behavior and skills or you wouldn't be here. The handbook is designed to enhance your skills and inform your behaviors.

The third element in this theme is courage. Often this consists of "speaking truth to power," a phrase attributed, variously, to the Quakers, to Islam, and to the Torah. In the context of your job as a presidential appointee, this kind of courage will require you to bring forward information that you believe is most relevant to dealing with the issue at hand regardless of whether those around you want to hear it. Challenging the conventional wisdom and testing the views of others is an element of courage that you must exhibit. This does not mean that you must continually be contrarian. Philosophers have stressed the need to have an ability to accept the things that cannot be changed, the courage to change the things that can be changed, and the wisdom to know the difference. Although often quoted, this is good advice for the appointee. This handbook will provide information about behaviors that can help you gain this wisdom.

Continual Learning

John Gardner says,

> Exploration of the full range of our own potentialities is not something that we can safely leave to the chances of life. It is something to be pursued avidly to the end of our days. We should look forward to an endless and unpredictable dialogue between our own potentialities and the claims of life—not only the claims we encounter, but the claims we invent. And by potentialities I mean not just skills, but the full range of our capacities for sensing, wondering, learning, understanding, loving, and aspiring.[4]

This definition of continual learning reflects the journey rather than the destination in acquiring new knowledge, skills, and abilities that mold our behavior. This handbook illuminates those competencies that have been important to other presidential appointees, gives you some perspective from people who have studied the issues carefully, and demonstrates why these competencies should be important aspects of your own behavior. However, it presupposes your commitment to being open to change and willing to foster positive change in your environment.

Informed Behavior

The handbook seeks to help you change your behavior by providing information on what you might need to serve the president and the nation. No book can give you everything you need to be successful. No book can give you motivation. If this handbook succeeds, it will give you some new ideas and help you use the documents and information contained here.

The Six Competencies

In part 1 of this handbook, a separate chapter is devoted to each of the six competencies listed at the beginning of this introduction. These chapters are designed to inform you about why the behavior in the competency is important, give you some advice from experts and people who have been in your position, and tell you how you might use the information to inform your own behavior.

There is a fine line between simply providing information and encouraging you to use it to change your behavior. During the administration of Lyndon B. Johnson, Joseph Califano was chosen to serve in the vitally important role of special assistant for domestic affairs. Given the fact that President Johnson intended to create a "Great Society," Califano was front and center in a major policy and legislative development effort. "It was my first time on the South Lawn of the White House, 1 a.m. on Tuesday July 13, 1965," remembers Califano. "As the President said good bye, he smiled. 'They tell me you're pretty smart, way up in your class at Harvard. Well, let me tell you something. What you learned on the streets of Brooklyn will be a damn sight more helpful to your president than anything you learned at Harvard.'"[5] Johnson was encouraging Califano to model his behavior on the rough and tumble world of Brooklyn rather than the academic setting of Cambridge. Califano thought enough of this advice to use it as the opening of his memoir.

While you may not get information about how to behave directly from the president, others who have served in prior administrations have given their views on the importance of the six competencies listed above. Throughout the handbook you will find their stories and lessons learned.

ONE

Leading for Results

As a presidential appointee you have come to Washington to get results—results that the president has promised the American people, results that the American people expect. Your job in achieving these results is, above all, leadership. You must inspire others. You must also help others set goals, track their progress toward meeting those goals, and measure their achievement.

To help you accomplish these tasks, a framework for management is essential. This framework will allow you to relate goals to measurable results. The process of measuring specific results has been refined and developed by many departments and agencies. The purpose of these efforts is to collect information that is useful for operating the agency, useful for overall management, and useful for meeting external reporting requirements.

The components of the leading for results competency are

—an accountability environment

—a method for measuring results, customer service, enablers, and public acceptance

—promotion of entrepreneurship and strategic thinking.

Accountability Environment

Forming an accountability environment in government is hard. Given government's perceived lack of a bottom line, program outputs or outcomes may not appear to be measurable. This perception is less true today than it was before the passage of the Government Performance and Results Act (GPRA) in 1993 and the introduction of the program assessment rating tool (PART).

While the executive branch has the primary responsibility for creating an accountability environment, under the Constitution, Congress has an important role to play in overseeing executive program accountability. Your agency environment should be designed to provide you useful information to manage and at the same time meet congressional oversight requirements simply and easily. Congress works through specific authorizing and oversight committees, using the hearing process to inform itself about the performance of specific programs and agency activities. Committees use this information both to encourage agencies to achieve better performance and to help them design legislation to make performance easier to achieve. At times oversight by Congress or by its accountability arm, the Government Accountability Office (GAO), may seem meddlesome or oppressive, but establishing a good relationship with the clerks of the relevant committees and with the GAO official in charge of your agency can smooth your path. And it is well to remember that the Constitution decrees that the Congress oversee executive activity.

In addition to congressional oversight and authorizing committees that are specific to your agency, the Senate Committee on Homeland Security and Governmental Affairs and the House Committee on Oversight and Government Reform have oversight government-wide of management areas such as civil service, accounting, procurement, reorganization of the executive branch, and information management.

The budget process—preparation, justification, and execution—is one of the most important management tools of the federal government and a central element in an accountability environment. In the budget process the work of the appropriations subcommittees often highlights accountability. Some agencies work with their appropriations subcommittees to align their legislatively required agency strategic planning process with the budgeting process. Where this alignment has happened, results have been brought into even clearer focus and duplication of agency efforts has been avoided.

The audience for results is not just those inside the government seeking to improve performance or having formal oversight responsibilities. For many public organizations there are also advocacy, lobbying, and interest groups that seek to examine the dealings and performance of government. Increasingly, transparency regarding results is being demanded by these groups. The media are continuously engaged in reviewing government action and results. Members of the general public are also keen to ensure responsiveness to their particular interests. It is clear that a successful leader must be able to respond to multiple constituencies with multiple instruments to demonstrate a command of an agency and its results.

An additional characteristic of accountability is the nature of agency responses to the analyses of independent parties such as the agency's inspector general and the GAO. The GAO continually monitors "high-risk areas," and agencies on this high-risk list are thought to be vulnerable to fraud, waste, abuse, and mismanagement.

In government, the integrity with which results are achieved is often as important for accountability as the results themselves. For example, on June 18, 2008, the GAO ruled that the $35 billion award to Northrop Grumman and the European Aeronautic Defence and Space Company (EAD) to build 179 midair refuelers to replace the current fleet had "a number of significant errors that could have affected the outcome of what was a close competition." The GAO further asserted that the Air Force had conducted "misleading and unequal discussions with Boeing."[1] Although the GAO did not formally comment on the substance of the decision, its commentary on the flawed process was an embarrassment to the Air Force and provides an important lesson in proper procurement procedure. In response, the Air Force has decided to rebid the contract, which will result in delay for the program.

An additional difficulty in measuring results is the question of what constitutes success. Unlike a *Fortune 500* CEO, who can demonstrate to shareholders and to the stock market that a firm's valuation is reliable and rising, a public servant cannot point to such measures, because there is no universal understanding in government of what success looks like. Often, the process seems more important than the results. Harvard scholar Graham Allison suggests that there are nine major differences between public and private organizations:[2]

—Time perspective: government managers have relatively short time horizons.

—Duration: tenure is relatively shorter for government managers.

—Measurement of performance: fewer standards exist for measuring performance.

—Personnel constraints: civil service systems, union contracts, and other regulations complicate personnel matters.

—Equity and efficiency: government places greater emphasis on equity among constituencies.

—Public versus private processes: governments tend to be exposed to more public scrutiny.

—Persuasion and direction: government managers mediate decisions in response to outside pressure.

—Legislative and judicial impact: government is more subject to scrutiny by legislative and judicial entities.

—Bottom line: government managers rarely have a clear bottom line.

However, some aspects of accountability in government are dominant: for example, there is an emphasis on the proper use of financial resources, on the ethical conduct of officials, and on fairness in business practices. To these must be added the broader concern of public support for government programs. As is well known, the public's opinion of the federal government has fallen in recent years, from 64 percent favorable in 2002 to 37 percent favorable in 2008.[3] Although this decline in public trust is often not about the results of government but about the actions of individuals, it has an overall corrosive effect.

Measuring Results: The Balanced Scorecard for Government

In the private sector the elements of an accountability environment are often tied together by a measurement framework called the balanced scorecard, which highlights the financial results that shareholders care about. The creators of the balanced scorecard describe these perspectives as follows:

F I G U R E 1-1. **Balanced Scorecard for Government**

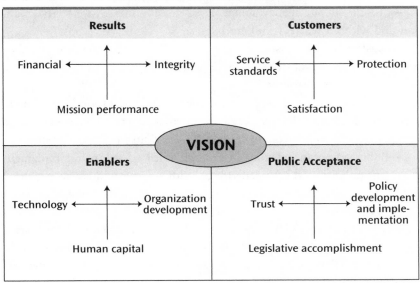

The balanced scorecard retains traditional financial measures. But financial measures tell the story of past events, an adequate story for industrial-
age companies for which investments in long-term capabilities and
customer relationships were not critical for success. These financial
measures are inadequate, however, for guiding and evaluating the journey that information-age companies must make to create future value
through investment in customers, suppliers, employees, processes, technology, and innovation.[4]

The version of the balanced scorecard I have designed for the public
sector is divided into four perspectives: results, customers, enablers, and
public acceptance (figure 1-1). Within each of the four perspectives three
metric categories allow both the manager and the public to know how the
agency is doing. These twelve metric categories allow for internal communications, particularly about operational issues, and external communications, particularly about meeting goals. All perspectives are informed
by their relationship to the overall vision of the agency. The vision is the
end state, the future that managers are trying to achieve.

The four perspectives address the following questions:

—Results: Is our agency achieving its mission in a cost-effective manner and without waste, fraud, and abuse?

—Customers: Are customer service standards being met and are they producing satisfied customers while protecting even customers unaware of their status as customers?

—Enablers: Are the workforce and the technological tools being used in a context of a modern learning organization that adapts to challenges? These are described in more detail in chapter 3, "Providing Technical Ability."

—Public acceptance: Is the government able to develop and implement coherent policies and get needed legislation passed in a timely fashion? Does the public trust the government to do the right things and to do them well?

The key to successful management in the public arena is to demonstrate to all stakeholders that each of the four quadrants is being continuously optimized in terms of achieving the agency's vision. But just defining and demonstrating success is not enough. The public has to accept that the vision is relevant to them and that the measures of success are things they care about. This acceptance requires simultaneous success in each of the four quadrants. One cannot be attended to at the expense of another.

The U.S. Office of Personnel Management describes an effective public leader as one who "has the ability to meet organizational goals and customer expectations." Inherent in this qualification "is the ability to make decisions that produce high-quality results by applying technical knowledge, analyzing problems, and calculating risks."[5] These high-quality results require working with your team to set clear goals and to define such results. The definition of results is often described in terms of activities undertaken, outputs produced, and outcomes achieved. James Q. Wilson describes these three categories as follows:

> Can the activities of their operators be observed? Can the results of those activities be observed? The first [question] involves *outputs*—what teachers, doctors, lawyers, engineers, police officers, and grant-givers do on a day-to-day basis. Outputs consist of the work the agency does. The second [question] involves *outcomes*—how, if at all, the world changes because of the outputs. Outcomes can be thought of as the results of agency work.[6]

Results Perspective

Some public managers are reluctant to be measured in terms other than activity and input. They argue that extraneous circumstances can affect outputs and outcomes; for example, meeting targets for clean outdoor air might be compromised by wildfires. However, although such extraneous circumstances do complicate outputs, the manager should allow for these circumstances. More often, managers fear that there will be negative actions taken if they fail to meet performance targets (especially if the failure is outside of their control). This fear makes it especially important to involve all managers in the development of goals, objectives, and measures.

All large agencies and many smaller ones in the federal government create strategic plans consistent with the Government Performance and Results Act of 1993. These plans are a good example for new appointees to follow when creating their own performance measures. Even though new policies from a new administration will mean the development of a new strategic plan and new measures of results, current strategic plans are helpful in the understanding of the overall form.

The current Environmental Protection Agency (EPA) strategic plan, for example, is an excellent template to follow.[7] The EPA has five broad goals: clean air, clean and safe water, land preservation and restoration, healthy communities and ecosystems, and environmental stewardship. Each of the goals has a set of objectives. The objectives for the first goal, for example, are healthier outdoor air, healthier indoor air, protection of the ozone layer, reduction of radiation, reduction of greenhouse gases, and enhanced scientific research. Table 1-1 shows a hypothetical performance report for the EPA goal for clean air and global climate change. Such a report is helpful to line managers and to their counterparts at regional and headquarters offices. For example, a detail from this hypothetical report regarding healthier outdoor air may show that South Florida monitoring stations report significantly higher ozone counts than usual. A resulting status risk is that the month's reading will lower the annual actual results. The following status issue arises: Can the wildfire monitoring station readings be removed to normalize the data?

A related objective to healthier outdoor air is a reduction in population-weighted ambient concentration of ozone. The long-term target is a

TABLE 1-1. Hypothetical Report, U.S. Environmental Protection Agency, Goal 1, Second Quarter, Fiscal Year 2008, by Stoplight Code

Objectives for Goal 1	Green	Red	Yellow	Total
Healthier outdoor air	1	1	0	2
Healthier indoor air	2	0	0	2
Protection of ozone layer	1	0	1	2
Reduction in radiation	2	0	0	2
Reduction in greenhouse gas emissions	2	0	0	2
Enhanced science and research	2	0	0	2

Detail from hypothetical "red" stoplight status report:
Name: 5/20 status&actual measurement
Date: 5/20/2008
Related objective: Objective 1.1: healthier outdoor air
Related target: FY 2008 population-weighted ambient ozone concentration in all monitored counties.
Target value: −8%
Actual value: −3%
Variance to target: 0.625
Description: South Florida monitoring stations are reporting ozone counts that are significantly higher than usual. This is likely due to wildfires in this part of the state.
Risks: There is a possibility that this month's reading will lower the annual actual results.
Issues: Can the wildfire monitoring station readings be removed to normalize the data?

reduction in this concentration by 14 percent by 2015. For the year measured in table 1-1 the target is 8 percent. How are we doing? Not so well: the actual reduction is only 3 percent. Wildfires in Florida have caused an increase in ozone, which is throwing off the aggregate results.

Thus data useful to line managers are collected and sent to more senior managers, where they are aggregated and used to measure progress on the objectives and goals of the agency. This kind of bottom-up, top-down approach involves all levels of management and creates a common frame of reference for performance. Robert Shea, former associate director of the Office of Management and Budget, has noted that the success of efforts like PART and ExpectMore will depend on the ability of the career staff at OMB to work with the next administration in refining and extending the reach of performance management.[8]

Financial integrity is another measure of results. Staying within budget and accounting for funds is extremely important. Deviations from budgets require an arduous reprogramming or legislative process that can be time consuming and subject to conflict. Similarly, failure to demonstrate that you have spent funds according to the budget and that you can account for the materials, supplies, and equipment that these funds purchased will create significant problems for your agency.

The same caveats exist for integrity in following the appropriate processes in both programs and administration. Such integrity could be considered another measurement of results. The public administration scholar Robert Behn argues that dependence on objective measurements has resulted in an accountability bias, putting a premium on financial accounting and ethics laws to the detriment of exceptional performance.[9] Poverty of ambition can develop, he says, which is a deterrent to risk taking in the interests of improving service and performance. As a presidential appointee, you will be asked to achieve results the administration cares about while ensuring that no process violations detract from these results. This balance is difficult to achieve.

Customer Service Perspective

For our purposes, the customers of government are those individuals or groups who have direct interaction with government. These individuals and groups range from Social Security beneficiaries to foreign corporations sending goods to the United States. In each case, there is a direct interaction—determining benefit eligibility, regulating lead content in toys—that should be governed by clearly understood standards of service.

Critical to providing good customer service are conducting surveys of customers' levels of satisfaction and using the results of these surveys to inform the way an agency is run. Starting in 1999 federal agencies were added to the University of Michigan's American Customer Satisfaction Index.[10] In 2007 the federal government had an ACSI score of 68; a sampling of agencies that scored well follows:

—Those responsible for interment, opinion of the National Cemetery Administration in the Veterans Administration: 95

—Inpatients opinion of TRICARE Medical Centers, Department of Defense: 89

—Retirees opinion of the Pension Benefit Guaranty Corporation: 88

—Users of the cancer information service of the National Cancer Institute, opinion of the National Institute of Health: 86

—Buyers of numismatic and commemorative coins, opinion of the U.S. Mint: 86

While these scores reflect only the attitudes of direct customers regarding particular federal programs, they provide valuable insights into how customer satisfaction measures can be used by government. Many agencies conduct their own analyses of customer attitudes and use them to redeploy resources or to change the process for delivering program activities.

For example, the Internal Revenue Service's survey of customer satisfaction, which measures many areas of its interaction with the public, has found a significant improvement in the satisfaction of paper filers.[11] Nonetheless, these filers' satisfaction lags in comparison to the satisfaction of electronic filers. Based partly on this kind of information, the IRS has made expanding the number of electronic filers a strategic objective.

Protection is another major area of customer service. Some individuals may be customers of the federal government but may not choose their time and place of interaction. Indeed, they may not be aware that they are customers. The intelligence community, for example, according to John McConnell, director of national intelligence, certainly views the public as its customer, particularly in regard to preserving civil liberties and privacy. We are "a unified enterprise of innovative intelligence professionals whose common purpose is defending American lives and interests, in advancing American values," he says, adding that the community performs its duties "under law in a manner that respects the civil liberties and privacy of all Americans."[12]

Public Acceptance Perspective

One of the most difficult things that governments do is measure public acceptance of the services that agencies provide. Finding effective and innovative ways to engage the public and ways to understand its acceptance of and even enthusiasm for a particular program or policy improves the public's trust in government. Trust is the essential ingredient for building overall support for the goals and objectives of an agency. Without trust, resources are more difficult to acquire, voluntary compliance is eroded, and internal morale suffers.

Much of the decline in public opinion of the federal government is related to public acceptance of the policies of an administration and the popularity of the president. For the individual agency, however, public acceptance is more related to the public's perception of the importance of the mission of the agency to their lives and the belief that the mission is being well executed. One of the keys to executing your agency's mission is to secure a strong legislative and regulatory framework and to keep that framework up to date.

For example, the Homeland Security Act of 2002 established the Department of Homeland Security (DHS) and made the Federal Emergency Management Agency (FEMA) a part of it. This legislative framework for FEMA has been both praised and criticized, especially in regard to the federal response to the Katrina disaster. In reaction to these and other criticisms, Congress, DHS, and FEMA created legislation and a set of policies and regulations governing disaster response. The Post-Katrina Emergency Management Reform Act of 2006 made the administrator of FEMA responsible for the management, maintenance, review, and revision of what was then called the National Response Plan. Part of this responsibility was exercised by the National Response Framework of 2008. Despite the problems of the past, the GAO recommended "that FEMA develop policies and procedures that guide how future revision processes will occur, particularly for collaborating with nonfederal stakeholders."[13]

Entrepreneurship and Strategic Thinking

David Osborne and Ted Gaebler subtitled their 1992 book on reinventing government, *How the Entrepreneurial Spirit Is Transforming the Public Sector.*[14] So the entrepreneurial spirit in government is not a new idea. But how does it work? Entrepreneurship in government involves developing innovations to existing management methods and administration to enhance an agency's performance. To this end, a leader may need to suspend long-standing operating procedures, give subordinates more leeway in management, and develop networks of cross-functional teams.

One proposal for achieving entrepreneurial vision was advanced by Harvard professor Mark H. Moore in his 1995 book *Creating Public Value.* Moore argues that public leaders should not simply carry on business as usual but should constantly review their mission and objectives and promote the maximum return on investment for the public. "Reflecting the winds of change in managerial thought," he says, "the managerial imagination strays beyond [its] traditional mandate, beyond [its] instinct for bureaucratic entrepreneurship . . . in imagining what could be done."[15] Imagining what could be done may involve creating new business processes, new partnerships, new client bases, and new methods. It may involve creating a way to measure the performance of an agency in terms of achieving change and the way these changes affect service quality and public satisfaction.

Strategic thinking is different from strategic planning. It is a cognitive approach that comes naturally for some but must be learned by others. One of the most creative and comprehensive definitions of strategic thinking is from the author Ingrid Bonn, who posits three attributes of a strategic thinker:[16]

—A holistic understanding of the organization and its environment, recognizing the linkages and complexity of the various substructures and relationships.

—The creativeness to rework old ideas and invent new ones.

—The ability to envision the future of the organization.

The five-star framework used by the University of Maryland's Burns Academy is one tool to help you think strategically about your organization and its effectiveness.[17] It consists of 125 questions, similar to those used in the Malcolm Baldridge National Quality Award, grouped into five areas:

—Analysis: Has the agency analyzed the hurdles to achieving its mission?

—Alignment: Are the agency's vision and strategy aligned?

—Action: Are the agency's plans for action helped by its organization and program structure?

—Accountability: What outcomes have been achieved? Are they consistent with the agency's objectives, goals, budget, and integrity?

—Acceptance: Do stakeholders value these outcomes? Do stakeholders agree with the agency policies that led to these outcomes?

A primary benefit of this survey is to start an organized dialogue among managers and co-workers that allows them to diagnose the current state of the agency and to prepare multiple prescriptions for dealing with weaknesses. The survey approach is sometimes called systems thinking, which

Peter Senge defines as "a discipline for seeing wholes . . . for seeing inter-relationships rather than things, for seeing patterns of change rather than static 'snapshots.'"[18]

An example of systems thinking in government occurred early in the process of reinventing the Internal Revenue Service. Stung by harsh criticism from Congress, Secretary of the Treasury Robert Rubin resolved to improve customer service at the IRS as part of a multidimensional effort to improve the agency's overall performance. Employee acceptance of change was critical to this improvement. Working with the National Treasury Employees Union, the Treasury working group ascertained that employees believed that the configuration of their computer desktops were inadequate for the task of answering inquiries quickly and adequately. While computer reconfiguration was not on its agenda for change, Treasury responded to this feedback from employees and altered desktop configurations. Two results occurred. First, employees felt they were consulted, which by itself improved performance. Second, the new desktop configuration resulted in quicker and more satisfying responses to customers.

One example of the power of strategic thinking comes from the period of the cold war, when the doctrine of mutual assured destruction formed the cognitive basis for the policies of the United States and its allies as well as for the policies of the Union of Soviet Socialist Republics. Thomas Schelling began to look at this doctrine to see if it could be put to a positive use. The 2005 Nobel Prize announcement tells the tale: "Schelling took on the complementary task of deducing the equilibria for interesting classes of games and evaluating whether these games and their equilibria were instructive regarding actual economic and social interaction. He did this against the background of the world's first nuclear arms race and came to contribute greatly to our understanding of its implications."[19] It has been said that Schelling's creation of a cognitive shift helped to stabilize the cold war.

Schelling's accomplishment might be called the epitome of leadership for results. As a presidential appointee, can you provide such leadership? Could this leadership stem the tide of non-state-sponsored terror? Combat the spread of AIDS? Solve the problems of urban crime?

TWO

Managing Change

Every four or eight years, a wave of new people, new ideas, and new policies arrive in the nation's capital. Changes occur at the highest level but also at the agency and subagency levels. Managing such change requires a knowledge of how to lead change or how to advise others who are leading it. Often this change comes in the form of innovation in policy or operations that require outside-of-the-box thinking, which is often hard to sell.

This chapter presents a framework for implementing change as well as a discussion of how to focus on innovation, including intuition and optimism—personal factors that enable the appointee to promote change and lead innovation. It is often difficult to use only one part of the brain (the practical process side) to meet complex challenges that present themselves in a nonlinear way and require creative thinking. Similarly, having a powerful optimism that is rooted in personal principles goes a long way toward motivating needed followers in the process of implementing change and spurring innovation.

Change Management: Kotter's Eight Factors

A leading analyst of change management, Harvard Business School professor John Kotter, lists eight factors necessary to implement change:[1] These factors have been revised slightly to reflect the unique challenges faced by presidential appointees:

—One: Establishing a sense of urgency
—Two: Creating a guiding coalition
—Three: Having a transforming vision
—Four: Communicating the vision
—Five: Removing obstacles to the vision
—Six: Planning for and creating short-term wins
—Seven: Guarding against declaring victory too soon
—Eight: Anchoring change in the organization's culture

Factor One: Establishing a Sense of Urgency

Establishing a sense of urgency—which some call a burning platform—requires leaders to communicate the impending crises or major challenges facing the agency. These communications can range from a presidential address to a video produced by a cabinet secretary. It is simple to pay lip service, even passionate lip service, to this step. People in your agency may try to wait out the new appointees and the sense of urgency they bring.

An example of resistance to change occurred when I was the chief financial officer at the Department of Housing and Urban Development (HUD). Secretary Henry Cisneros asked me to visit all ten regional offices and several area offices as part of a reorganization effort. This was the third or fourth reorganization in the past four years, and people in the field were cynical. Despite the fact that many former HUD officials were being indicted and the entire department had been placed on the GAO high-risk list—the only department to ever be so designated—there was no coalition for change. I would like to be able to say that my own efforts spurred major transformation. That was not the case. Transformation came from bold policy initiatives by the secretary, the Federal Housing Administration commissioner, the assistant secretary for public and Indian housing, and the assistant secretary for community planning and development. The one thing I can take credit for is helping to create an organizational structure that centralized overall responsibility for program results in headquarters.

In each of the HUD programs slated for change, business as usual was shown to be the wrong way to go. For example, in public housing, the burning platform was the terrible condition of public housing units all across America. From Cabrini Green in Chicago to East Falls in Philadelphia people were living in horrible circumstances. These conditions were summarized by Secretary Cisneros: "Many of the older big city projects have become environments of such sheer terror that local housing authorities are willing to try almost any technique, including defensible space, to alleviate the nightmare." Ultimately, defensible space would not be enough, and Cisneros led the charge to demolish these places, where "residents have become prisoners in their own apartments, cringing behind darkened windows, and hoping to avoid random sprays of gunfire."[2]

The case was made to Congress, HUD employees, and public officials that massive change was needed. This plea was coupled with carrots and sticks. The carrots were new programs that Congress approved, such as Hope VI, and the sticks were federal takeovers of local housing authorities. The success of this transformation can be seen across the nation today in terms of new housing units in revitalized communities.

Factor Two: Creating a Guiding Coalition

In creating a coalition, the appointee must manage up, down, and sideways. Managing up entails getting the most senior agency leadership to prioritize the change. It also requires acceptance of the change by the White House. The president's direct staff—often constituted in one of the White House policy councils—needs to be convinced, as does the Office of Management and Budget staff. Even when the administration is ready to sign on, relevant congressional staff and congressional members themselves must be persuaded that the proposed change is valuable to the American people.

The sideways part comes in getting commitment from counterparts within your agency and from stakeholders in other agencies and outside the government. An example of this was the International Trade Data System (ITDS). This program was conceived in 1993 by a small group of agencies that dealt with international trade issues. The group believed that common data standards for shippers and forwarders would streamline the trade process, provide better data, and help them meet their individual missions. It proved an extremely difficult coalition to build.

As it developed, ITDS became a loose network of more than ninety gov-ernment agencies, each with a set of data requirements based in law and regulation, requirements that needed to be harmonized. Domestic and for-eign elements of private industry and government agencies all needed to participate if the project was to be successful. A trade support network had to be created to provide input into the design of data standards and systems. As ITDS was being created, Congress approved a new computer system for the U.S. Customs Service called the Automated Commercial Environment (ACE) project. Although this project was potentially a bless-ing for ITDS, it came at a price. The ACE project had not fully bought into the principles of ITDS; the guiding coalition—whose only charter was a memorandum from Vice President Al Gore—had to reform itself within the context of the larger effort. Only the strong leadership of chair Eugene Rosengarden kept the effort together and focused.

Rosengarden's ability to manage across this broad coalition as well as the U.S. Customs Service, Congress, and the OMB led to the success of the program. This success is reflected in the following quotation from the deputy OMB director for management, Clay Johnson, to all federal agency heads:

> On July 18, 2007, the President issued Executive Order 13439 to review and assess current import safety procedures and methods, survey the authorities and practices of federal agencies, and outline preliminary steps necessary to enhance the safety of imported products. A strategic framework to improve import safety has been developed based on this review and assessment. By mid-November a follow-on action plan based on this framework will lay out a road map with short- and long-term recommendations for improving import safety. One of the imme-diate approved action items recommended by the working group is to require use of the International Trade Data System (ITDS) when col-lecting information to clear or license the import and export of cargo. ITDS is being implemented as part of the Automated Commercial Envi-ronment (ACE) project, U.S. Customs and Border Protection's new import and export processing system.[3]

Thus ITDS became the system of choice for agencies seeking to enhance product safety. And even though the system by itself is not enough to ensure product safety, it represents a networked approach that may be a guide for the future.

Factor Three: Having a Transforming Vision

Real change is transformational. Pulitzer Prize–winning author James MacGregor Burns defines the leader's role in transformational change as follows: "Creative leadership reframes values above all. . . . Its vision of what might be is grounded in the fulfillment of a moral purpose."[4] Burns goes on to cite the "value creation" of Theodore Roosevelt's vision regarding the conservation ethic as a prime example of transformational leadership. Invoking the Constitution as a basis for the creation of "united action in the wise use of our national resources," Roosevelt convened a governor's conference that included all state and territorial governors, almost his entire cabinet, all nine justices of the Supreme Court, representatives of professional societies, and nearly 400 individuals representing all aspects of conservation.[5] Clearly TR was building a guiding coalition toward his vision of transformational change in the conservation of resources and lands.

The agenda had ninety-five aspects of conservation, grouped under eleven headings. In his invocation, Roosevelt stated that conservation was "the chief material question that confronts us, second only—and second always—to the great fundamental question of morality." The creation of the National Park System and a new legislative agenda were the results of this transformation. To achieve these results, Roosevelt needed the coalition he created through the governor's conference.

Although few presidential appointees have the opportunity to participate in such a sweeping transformation, each administration has objectives that can be called transformational. Your role may be to help develop the vision for these objectives or it may be to translate that vision into results.

Factor Four: Communicating the Vision

John Kotter suggests that a prime weakness in implementing change is not wholly communicating the vision, and he supplies a recipe: "Transformation is impossible unless hundreds and thousands of people are willing to help, often to the point of making short-term sacrifices. Employees will not make sacrifices, even if they are unhappy with the status quo, unless they believe that useful change is possible. Without credible communication, and a lot of it, hearts and minds of the troops are never captured."[6]

The National Performance Review (NPR), headed by Vice President Al Gore, was masterful at communicating its vision. The vice president lent his bully pulpit to the effort. An example of his success was his appearance on the David Letterman television show wearing goggles and wielding a hammer, which he used to smash an ashtray. He was demonstrating the foolishness of regulations that required that ashtrays contain only a certain number of pieces when broken. The public was so taken with the hammer segment that the NPR adopted it as a symbol and presented "hammer awards" to programs that demonstrated the NPR values of cutting red tape and creating a government that "works better and costs less."

Factor Five: Removing Obstacles to the Vision

At the beginning of the transformation process, the number of obstacles is often greater than the ability to remove them one by one. Having a strong vision certainly helps, and communication of the vision empowers more and more of the stakeholders as time goes on. Still, there need to be wholesale methods to remove obstacles.

The President's Management Agenda, created by President George W. Bush in 2002, identifies these obstacles as follows: "Though reform is badly needed, the obstacles are daunting—as previous generations of would-be reformers have repeatedly discovered. The work of reform is continually overwhelmed by the constant multiplication of hopeful new government programs, each of whose authors is certain that this particular idea will avoid the managerial problems to which all previous government programs have succumbed."[7] Bush's prescription was freedom to manage: "Federal managers are greatly limited in how they can use available financial and human resources to manage programs; they lack much of the discretion given to their private sector counterparts to do what it takes to get the job done. Red tape still hinders the efficient operation of government organizations; excessive control and approval mechanisms afflict bureaucratic processes. Micromanagement from various sources— congressional, departmental, and bureau—imposes unnecessary operational rigidity."[8] This approach gave Bush administration appointees and their senior management colleagues the ability to remove obstacles to implementing the president's vision for a government that is "active but limited, that focuses on priorities and does them well."

Factor Six: Planning for and Creating Short-Term Wins

Sustaining the attention of an organization is more likely to occur if there are signs of quick progress. The President's Management Agenda uses a color-coded chart to portray the status of management initiatives. An initiative whose status moves along the color spectrum allows agency heads to celebrate progress even before reaching the ultimate goal.

Factor Seven: Guarding against Declaring Victory Too Soon

The phrase "Mission accomplished!" has taken on the meaning of a premature declaration of victory. It is likely that the Pentagon and President Bush wish now that those words had not been inscribed on the banner flying over the *USS Lincoln* on that day in May 2003 when the president spoke about victory in Iraq. It was, in fact, only the end of the beginning of the war, not the beginning of the end (to paraphrase Churchill). Another premature declaration, "Peace in our time," by Neville Chamberlain, is famous for vastly underestimating the effort it would take to contain, combat, and defeat Adolf Hitler. It is hard enough to establish the burning platform, create the coalition, define the vision, and so on without declaring the end only to find that there is another mountain range to cross.

Factor Eight: Anchoring Change in the Organization's Culture

Organizational culture is "the deeper level of basic assumptions and beliefs that are learned responses to the group's problems of survival in its external environment and its problems of internal integration." These assumptions and beliefs "are shared by members of an organization, operate unconsciously, and define . . . an organization's view of itself and its environment."[9] This definition of organizational culture by Massachusetts Institute of Technology professor Edgar Schien stresses its influence; in fact, Schien equates an organization's culture with its survival. Unless change agents recognize this and embed change in the institutional culture, change is unlikely to survive.

In 1993, as part of an effort called OMB 2000, the White House Office of Management and Budget set out to more fully integrate the M (management) into the OMB. At first those in the management offices resisted the idea that their work would be carried out by people on the budget side of the organization. However, these former budget analysts (now program analysts) have proven themselves to be stalwart allies in institutionalizing management reform, as can be seen in the success of the President's Management Agenda and the program assessment rating tool (PART). This change in culture has created an integration in OMB that few thought possible.

An example of the workings of this change in the OMB culture came in the OMB response to the year 2000 (Y2K) computer challenge. Many experts feared that fundamental flaws in older computers would render them useless at the millennium because they would fail to recognize a new date convention that started with twenty rather than nineteen. Under the direction of a special assistant to the president, John Koskinen, the budget and management sides of OMB developed agency plans and allocated more than $2 billion to the effort. The management component—the Office of Information and Regulatory Affairs—and the various budget associate directors and deputy associate directors ensured that each federal agency was ready when the millennial moment occurred. They also guaranteed that Koskinen had the support within the agencies to stimulate the private sector to anticipate its own problems.

Innovation

According to the management guru Peter Drucker, innovation is "change that creates a new dimension of performance."[10] Harvard professor and one-time presidential appointee Elaine Kamarck tells us that the role of innovation in government and the motivation of individuals to initiate and carry out innovation and reform are different from those in the public sector:

> Innovation is not easy. In the private sector and in the public sector innovation disrupts established relationships and behaviors. Innovation, therefore, requires imagination and courage. But in the private sector innovation can often result in large financial rewards and greater market share. Thus people in the private sector have tended to value, promote, and invest in innovation. This is largely not so in the public sector. The financial rewards from successful innovation are likely to accrue to the State, not to the individuals involved in the innovation. And since the public sector has traditionally been a monopoly provider of many goods and services, people in the public sector have had little incentive to engage in, much less invest in, innovation.[11]

The process of innovation is defined in a variety of ways and can focus on a range of problems, from individual creativity to organizational adaptability. Trial and error are essential to the process, as is thinking outside of the box. For the presidential appointee this may be difficult. If policies from the top are clear and the problem is well defined, finding an innovative solution is easier. If there is lack of clarity in these areas, the first step is to go back to the beginning and seek to create consensus on what changes are needed to solve the problems. If innovation is "change that creates a new dimension of performance," then it is important to define success at the outset. A clear definition of the problem, a clear vision of future success, and a clear measure of success are all essential.

The burning platform of public housing projects is described above. These federally funded, locally operated housing projects became centers of dysfunctional social behavior and neighborhood blight during the 1980s and 1990s. Secretary of Housing and Urban Development Henry Cisneros set out to change that. He built a coalition of people from the federal government, Congress, advocacy groups, local governments, and public housing authorities whose aim was to find a new approach to the fundamental mission of housing the poor. The new approach was called the Hope VI program; changes wrought by the Hope VI program were such that in 2000 the Ash Institute of Harvard University's Kennedy School of Government presented an innovation-in-government award to the Hope VI program, noting that "Hope VI public housing is generating a new level of civic culture and is serving as an engine for neighborhood renewal."[12]

Often, to be innovative, individuals must be freed from day-to-day responsibility for some period of time. With this freedom comes the opportunity to focus on the task and to make dramatic leaps forward. An example of such innovation is the CIA's and the Air Force's close working relationship with the ultrasecret Lockheed Skunk Works, a small group of engineers, designers, and machinists working on "technologically advanced airplanes for highly secret missions," according to Ben Rich, the second head of the Skunk Works.[13] "What came off our drawing boards provided key strategic and technological advantages for the United States, since our enemies had no way to stop our overflights." Rich describes the innovative process that produced an aircraft that was "a thousand times less visible":

> As it happened, I was damned lucky. Stealth technology landed in my lap—a gift from the gods assigned to take care of beleaguered executives, I guess. I take credit for immediately recognizing the gift I was handed before it became apparent to everyone else, and for taking major risks in expending development costs before we had any real government interest or commitment. The result was that we produced the most significant advance in military aviation since the jet engine, rendering null and void the enormous 300-billion-ruble investment the Soviets had made in missile and radar defenses over the years. No matter how potent their missiles or powerful their radar, they could not shoot down what they could not see.

The themes here of luck, recognition, and investment provide lessons for the presidential appointee. Seeking out and being open to innovation, which may or may not present itself, can give you the opportunity to develop new solutions to complex problems. Both the organization and the individual must have the flexibility to see new ways of dealing with old problems. They must also act in accordance with their values and those promulgated by the president. For example, during the Great Depression,

Franklin Roosevelt called for "bold, persistent experimentation." He believed that "it is common sense to take a method and try it. If it fails, admit it frankly and try another. But above all try something."[14] This approach gave those in the Roosevelt administration permission to try new approaches and even to fail.

Other administrations have had a more conservative vision of their role. President George W. Bush saw a role for his administration in protecting the prerogatives of the presidency. This approach requires presidential appointees to adapt their behavior and that of their organizations to resisting encroachment by Congress and others as they seek to implement innovative policies.

Intuition

The formal processes of planning and consultation are not always available to the presidential appointee. Many decisions need to be made on the spot and, as Harvard Divinity School professor Harvey Cox has been paraphrased, not to decide is to decide.[15] Innovative action is often based on informed intuition. As an example of this, the best-selling author Malcolm Gladwell recounts the choices that have to be made on the battlefield in the time of war and quotes Marine Corps general Paul Van Riper:

> When we talk about analytic versus intuitive decision making, neither is good or bad. What is bad is if you use either of them in an inappropriate circumstance. Suppose you had a rifle company pinned down by machine-gun fire. And the company commander calls his troops together and says, "We have to go through the command staff with the decision making process." That's crazy. He should make a decision on the spot, execute it, and move on.[16]

An extension of this approach using modern technology is described by Marine Corps brigadier general Jerry McAbee in discussing the relationship between technology and intuition. McAbee says that virtual reality training and simulation systems have given the military a glimpse into the future but that new technology is needed to complete the vision. "Instead of trying to deliver a perfect picture of the battlefield, we need to shift from that, because the battlefield is chaotic and commanders are trained early on in their careers to make decisions based on their experience, intelligence, and intuition." He says that people make decisions differently: "One shoe doesn't fit all. We need to tailor that stimuli. I think it will be incremental, and we may never [fully] develop the system, but we need to start down that road . . . to assist commanders in intuitive decisionmaking."[17]

Optimism

A companion to intuition is optimism. In the dark days of World War II, Winston Churchill had much to be pessimistic about. However, he chose to be a beacon of optimism despite his own self-doubt and demons. A quotation attributed to Churchill sums up his approach: "A pessimist sees the difficulty in every opportunity; an optimist sees the opportunity in every difficulty."[18]

At the very top of American government we find examples of optimism. The journalist David Shribman describes Franklin Roosevelt's optimism as "allowing him to beat the Depression and the Axis powers." He continues: "A pessimist would have shrunk from either challenge. So might a realist; one out of every four Americans who wanted to work was without a job when FDR became president in 1933, and Germany and Japan were in the ascendant when the United States entered World War II in 1941."[19]

THREE

Providing Technical Ability

All presidential appointees coming into a new administration have their own specific skill sets. Some may be accountants, others policy specialists, and others political or communications specialists. Technical knowledge and the ability to apply it are central to an appointee's role in the administration. Each agency and office is seeking to attract talented individuals who can contribute to the mission of the organization. To make this task easier, databases are created by the Office of Presidential Personnel that highlight the technical skills needed and those available. While political and policy considerations are always important, technical competence is often the key to appointment.

Having technical knowledge and ability at the outset of your appointment is not enough, however. Continual improvement in technical knowledge and ability is imperative for the following reasons:

—Your agency benefits from your increased skills.

—You add to the administration's cadre of competent leaders.

—You can undertake increasingly higher levels of responsibility.

—You can undertake new assignments.

My own experience is a case in point. I came to the Clinton administration as the chief financial officer of the Department of Housing and Urban Development. After about eighteen months I was asked to move to the Office of Management and Budget as controller. My final job at

OMB was as deputy director for management. My tenure in the federal government was about six years. It could seem that I did not provide continuity, since I moved three times. In reality, the skills learned at one level allowed me to be more effective at the next and to continue to supply oversight and assistance to those taking my old positions. This is similar to rotation in the military sector and promotion in the private sector.

Four technical skills are crucial to you as you begin your job:

—Financial management

—Human capital management

—Procurement management

—Technology management

Many highly successful presidential appointees will arrive with specific background in a particular policy, regulatory, or operational area. Participating in communities of interest, reading the current press, listening to scholars and to other practitioners, taking all available training, and attending relevant conferences will also help to expand your domain knowledge. Additional training—in the federal role in housing, health care, and national security, for example—may be available only after you are on the job. Unfortunately, federal training programs fall short of the ideal.

Michael Mears, a former human resources professional with the Central Intelligence Agency who also has worked in the private sector, notes the severe shortfalls generally in federal executive training: "Excluding the military. . . the quantity of leadership training never reaches critical mass. . . . I would like to see an absolute minimum of five student days of leadership training each year for anyone in supervisory, management, or executive positions."

Mears goes on to categorize training as "three buckets: administration (such as managing budgets and contracts), management (solving problems, implementing), and leadership (inspiring people to higher performance levels)." Without additional training in these areas, Mears says, "government executives don't have the skills and tools, and therefore don't have the confidence to attack what's obvious: too much bureaucracy, low levels of organizational trust, and employee disempowerment."

Financial Management

Financial management in the federal government can be divided into three processes: budget preparation, budget execution, and accounting and reporting. All budgeting and financial management in the federal government is based on these three processes. Unlike the private sector and state and local government, where such functions as cash management, debt issuance, and investment play a role in management decisions even at the line level, in the federal government these functions are the responsibilities of the U.S. Department of the Treasury. Proper financial management requires planning, execution, and accounting/internal control at the agency level. The common frame of reference for accountability is the agency's budget. Allocation, distribution, and results can all be measured in terms of this budget.

Important to the budget preparation stage of financial management is learning your agency's budgetary policies and procedures in the context of overall presidential and congressional budget policies and procedures. Building a relationship with the resource management offices of the Office of Management and Budget is therefore important, since this office seeks to carry out the overall policies of the administration on an agency-by-agency basis and can help you align your agency's programs with overall policy. Specific measures such as the program assessment rating tool (PART) can help you juxtapose performance and finances to determine whether a particular program is meeting its objective in a cost-effective manner.[1] And guidance also is offered through OMB Circular A-11.

As for the relation of your agency's budget to the overall budget, it is well to keep in mind that three budget processes happen simultaneously in the federal government. In calendar year 2008, for example, the budget for fiscal year 2008 is being executed, the budget for fiscal year 2009 is being defended, and the budget for fiscal year 2010 is being defined.

Budget execution faithful to the president's policies and within the context of congressional appropriation is a core task of presidential appointees. The OMB works with agencies during the execution, and it may from time to time use an apportionment and allotment mechanism to achieve presidential and congressional intent as interpreted by the OMB.[2]

As an appointee you have to see that the pace of spending is moderate—neither outpacing results nor slowing them down—and demonstrate that the expenditure of funds is producing results. Many federal agencies have adopted integrated financial management systems, which provide continual updates on both program data and financial data. Understanding these systems will help you manage programs and avoid internal control problems.

The two important aspects of accounting are reporting and internal control. Reporting allows you to present fairly the financial condition of the agency. However, Grant Thornton partners Clifton Williams and Morgan Kinghorn indicate that surveys of federal leaders in 2006 and 2007 show that few people read audited financial statements and fewer still use them for budget and business decisions.[3] As shown in box 3-1, they recommend a reporting model that links performance and financial information from the operational level to decisionmakers.

The principles and rules governing internal controls are of two types: government-wide and agency-specific. These rules, regulations, and policies are in place to help avoid waste, fraud, and abuse and to lay down best practices for financial and program execution.[4] Failure to follow these practices could land your program on the Government Accountability Office's high-risk list.

Contrary to fears, programs do get off the high-risk list. For example, the single-family mortgage program and the rental housing assistance program at the Department of Housing and Urban Development, which were placed on the list in 1994, were removed in 2007. As the presidentially appointed chief financial officer at HUD, I was aware of the failings of internal controls in these programs. It took many years of hard work over two administrations to satisfy the GAO that the shortcomings of these programs had been remedied. I learned from this experience that the fact that I was not responsible for the initial problem did not prevent me from bearing responsibility for fixing the problem. My advice to new appointees is to treat the reports of the inspector general with seriousness and to use auditors' reports on weaknesses in management control as guides for corrective action.

Human Capital Management

The federal civil service system, with employment based on merit, was created by President Theodore Roosevelt and others in response to the spoils

BOX 3-1. Accounting and Accountability: Next Steps for Government

Clifton A. Williams and C. Morgan Kinghorn of Grant Thornton LLP

A congressional committee wants you to testify next week on the cost effectiveness of your federal agency's services. Your deputy brings in last fiscal year's performance and accountability report (the PAR). In it are more than 50 pages of the agency's audited annual financial statements and 100 pages of performance measures. Both the financial and performance data go into minute detail. Though detailed, the data are not the agency mission, "bang for the buck" results you would like to show lawmakers. And by the way, the committee would like proof that data are reliable and accurate. Looks like you, your staff, and the agency division heads had better cancel weekend plans—time for a marathon data call.

Each year, the federal government spends millions of dollars to prepare and audit annual financial statements that few people read. Battalions of bureaucrats collect reams of performance measures that decisionmakers will never use. In 2008, though, a new way of looking at government costs and results emerged that promises to truly integrate performance and financial reporting, increase transparency, and improve public service. It is called *performance-based management and accounting*.

Wrong structure for financial and performance reporting?

The Chief Financial Officers Act of 1990 (the CFO Act) requires most large federal entities to have annual audited financial statements like those used by corporations. The Government Performance and Results Act of 1993 (GPRA) requires, among other things, that agencies measure and report their performance. The Reports Consolidation Act of 2000 resulted in OMB combining financial and performance reports into an annual performance and accountability report (the PAR).

Surveys of federal CFOs and other financial leaders in 2006 and 2007 show that few people read audited financial statements and fewer still use them for budget and business decisions. Other than being bound into the same volume, there is no clear or consistent link between financial reports and performance reports.

Developing a better structure

An ideal model for decisionmaking would let users link performance and financial information. It would allow the easy movement of data from lower to higher levels of operations and, vice versa, would facilitate drilling down into operations to search for root causes of problems and determining possible solutions. Finally, the model would show the reliability of its information. Performance-based management and accounting can do all these things and is the next logical step in federal performance management.

Performance-based management and accounting is a multidimensional measurement approach that arrays existing financial data into a process view. Processes are how work is done in an entity. Performance-based management and accounting aligns financial reporting with an entity's business operations and processes, outputs and outcomes. Most federal entities today practice some form of process-based analysis for program delivery. Adding a process focus to financial reporting enhances this management approach.

system, which had corrupted federal employment. The civil service is meant to be a bulwark against favoritism in hiring. It has its critics, though—those who believe that merit-based hiring is slow and discourages qualified applicants.[5] In response to these critics and others, pay-for-performance experiments are being undertaken in the federal employment system. A prescription for change in this area is contained in the recently released "Roadmap to Reform," from Partnership for Public Service.

Beyond recruitment and retention, the federal government faces challenges in integrating the performance of individuals and their agencies with the pay and incentive systems. In January 2007 the management of human capital was still on the GAO's high-risk list, meaning that this area was not meeting expectations.

> GAO first added strategic human capital management as a government-wide high-risk area in 2001 because federal agencies lacked a strategic approach to human capital management that integrates human capital efforts with agency mission and program goals. The area remains high risk because the federal government now faces one of the most significant transformations to the civil service in half a century, as momentum grows toward making government-wide changes to agency pay, classification, and performance management systems.
>
> Moving forward, there is still a need for a government-wide framework to advance human capital reform in order to avoid further fragmentation within the civil service, ensure management flexibility as appropriate, allow a reasonable degree of consistency, provide adequate safeguards, and maintain a level playing field among federal agencies competing for talent. Agencies must continue to assess their workforce needs and make use of available authorities. Congress should make pay and performance management reform the first step in any government-wide reform effort, and the Office of Personnel Management (OPM) should evaluate and learn from its approach to implementing the performance-based pay system for senior executives and apply these lessons to future human capital reforms.[6]

The GAO notes that modern, effective, economical, and efficient human capital practices, policies, and procedures—integrated with mission and program goals—are central to transforming federal agencies into results-oriented, high-performing organizations. Indeed, human capital reforms, accompanied by safeguards to help ensure they are implemented fairly and effectively, can pay dividends through more efficient agency operations.[7]

How is this advice relevant to you as a presidential appointee? Two findings of the Partnership for Public Service's survey of chief human capital officers highlight the appointees' role. One finding is that senior leadership is the key to success in changing human capital practices. The second finding is that attention from the White House motivates senior leaders. Given the spotlight that the GAO has turned on this issue, it is likely that the 2009 high-risk report will set forth a continuing challenge for the new administration.

The problem of talent management is not limited to the federal government. A 2006 survey of CEOs found that "companies view the ability to manage talent effectively as a strategic priority. Yet our research finds that senior executives largely blame themselves and their business line managers for failing to give the issue enough time and attention. They also believe that insular 'silo' thinking and a lack of collaboration across the organization remain considerable handicaps."[8]

One way for presidential appointees to avoid the silo mentality is to actively participate in and follow the work of the various communities of interest in the federal government. Depending on your level of appointment and interest, groups such as the President's Management Council, the Chief Acquisition Officers Council, the Chief Financial Officers Council, the Chief Human Capital Officers Council, and the Chief Information Officers Council can help you network with career leaders as well as other appointees. Even if you are not eligible for membership in these organizations, reviewing their websites from time to time will keep you aware of the challenges and initiatives in these areas.[9]

Procurement Management

The former administrator of the Office of Federal Procurement Policy, who is now at Harvard, Steven Kelman, suggests that for many agencies, "contracting management must be considered a core competence of the organization," since contracting represents a major part of many agencies' budgets.[10] In fiscal year 2006, for example, the government paid contractors over $400 billion.[11] Thus, the sheer size of such procurement makes it an important focus for the appointee. The following analysis of the military's contracting activities in Iraq and Afghanistan is a case in point:

> History shows that whatever threats the army next faces will be different from the last, but they are likely to be expeditionary and likely to involve high numbers of contractor personnel. At the same time, operating the most potent military force of all time carries with it the burden that nothing is as simple as it once was. Our armed forces have been stretched thin. Technology has changed. All of our military services now use contractors to provide essential services. What has not changed is that contracting with taxpayers' funds is an inherently governmental function, and the military commander needs competent professional advice in the exercise of the expeditionary contracting mission.[12]

The core observation here is that contracting with taxpayers' money is "an inherently governmental function." This means that it must be overseen by senior government employees charged with protecting the financial and programmatic interest of the federal government. As a presidential appointee, you have a special role in promoting good contracting, avoiding bad contracting, and knowing the difference. Since the beginning of government, scandals have plagued public officials.[13] It is highly likely that they will occur in the new administration. What to do? Read congressional history, read GAO reports, read inspector general reports. Representative Henry Waxman, chair of the House Committee on Oversight and Government Reform, had this to say in a 2007 speech: "For the first time annual federal procurement spending crossed the $400 billion threshold, and more than half of this spending—over $200 billion in new contracts—was awarded without full and open competition. . . . We identified 187 contracts that federal auditors have found to be plagued by wasteful spending or mismanagement. The cumulative value of these problem contracts is now over $1 trillion."[14]

It is incumbent, then, on presidential appointees with contracting responsibility to follow certain procedures:

—Analyze the procurement execution and oversight process.

—Determine the skill levels of individuals who carry out the procurement function and the support they are receiving from senior management.

BOX 3-2. Thoughts from the Field

Stan Z. Soloway, President, Professional Services Council

My thoughts are founded on my belief that very few presidential appointees (or career senior managers, for that matter) recognize the significance of procurement to their agency operations or have any real understanding of how government procurement works. Government-wide, contracting now occupies some 40 percent of the discretionary budget (in services alone it is almost 25 percent). I would argue that it must be a key focus of any senior presidential appointee, since agency mission success is increasingly tied to procurement and contracts. One could argue whether in some discreet areas contracting is too ubiquitous, but I think such arguments miss the point. Contracting is a fact of life, and the reality is that for the foreseeable future it will continue to be a fact of life and in fact become even more important. With that in mind, I offer the following five thoughts.

1. Appointees should meet early with their agency's procurement leadership and get a full, data-driven briefing on the role of contracting in the agency, including a breakdown of spending on products, hardware, and services—as well as a further breakdown on the types of services involved. The review should go a step further as well: appointees should ask both their inspector general and their procurement executive to provide a confidential high-risk briefing. This should result in a collective discussion to achieve alignment over where the biggest gaps or problems are. The briefings or discussions should also include a review of the training funds available for the acquisition workforce and the professional development plans that are in place.

2. Appointees should dedicate at least a day during their transition to an understanding of acquisition. They need not become acquisition experts, but they do need to understand the lingo and the general processes involved. Moreover, they should be knowledgeable enough so they are not unduly swayed by—and can effectively deal with people who are swayed by—the myths about contracting. This includes such myths as the so-called shadow

---

—Talk to the entire contracting community, including potential vendors, about the fairness and cost effectiveness of the contracting process. Groups such as the Professional Services Council can provide useful insights. The council's president, Stan Soloway, offers five "thoughts from the field" to presidential appointees (see box 3-2).[15]

workforce and the so-called competition. This primer must be fact based and devoid of bias in either direction. It should also include some discussion of the changes made to the system during the Clinton administration and of why they were made.

3. Initial program reviews should include information on, for example, the prime contractors involved and their performance histories. Too many appointees do not even know what their major programs are, let alone who is responsible for them.

4. Appointees should make explicit (and regular) overtures to their acquisition workforce. These are the journeyman frontliners who are charged with making the agency work. Yet they have often not been granted the stature or support their roles require and deserve. For example, in 1998, in the face of the so-called spare parts scandal, Secretary Bill Cohen, in a broadcast to the entire Defense Department, said that he was receiving demands from Capitol Hill to fire the people responsible. He resisted this call and then went on to say that he was nevertheless committed to figuring out what went wrong and why. He wanted people to "think more about being innovative than about being punished for making honest mistakes." That simple statement resonated throughout the department and is still occasionally cited today. In simple terms, if we are asking the acquisition workforce to execute so many elements of the government's complex missions, they need to feel supported. Presidential appointees set the tone for how much tolerance there will be for error and how much real impetus there will be for innovation. As basic as it sounds, this is a tone and theme that is often lacking.

5. Ensure that your senior procurement executive is on your senior management team and a full participant in agencywide strategic and management activities, which also involve the chief human capital officer, the chief financial officer, and the chief information officer.

Technology Management

The Office of Personnel Management lists as an executive core qualification, "Makes effective use of technology to achieve results," clearly assuming that the executive is at least conversant with technology.[16] With the ongoing convergence of technology, business processes, and organizational design, this assumption is more and more relevant. The effective and innovative use of technology can mean success in program implementation. This is especially true as ever tighter budgets require more cost-effective ways of doing business. The Ford Foundation/Kennedy School Award program for innovation in government lists large numbers of winners and finalists in agencies that are driven by technology.[17]

Modern technology also includes data security and system security. The threat of attacks by hackers seeking to gain access to an agency's information base makes such security a high priority for the appointee. Alan Paller, president of the SANS Institute, who has been involved in helping agencies cope with cyberspace attacks, offers the following advice for appointees:[18]

—Identify individuals personally responsible for each federal information technology asset.

—Require these individuals to report regularly on the implementation of each security program.

—Ensure that the inspector general is supportive of the security programs.

Beyond the agencies' own use of technology, collaborative tools such as Web 2.0 enable appointees to leverage their agency's mission by incorporating processes and practices that have been successful in other areas.

FOUR

Leading Others

One standard management text defines leadership as follows: "Leadership is the process by which one individual influences others to accomplish desired goals."[1] This definition has been countered by others. James MacGregor Burns says that there are two potential sets of goals: transactional and transformational; Daniel Goleman says that leadership is primal; Warren Bennis and Burt Nanus say that leadership is about trust.[2] They are all right. Cataloging the aspects of leadership is a complex study in itself.

The Jepson School of Leadership at the University of Richmond, a major center for leadership studies, defines the method of teaching this discipline as follows: "To teach for and about leadership, the school uses the multiple-disciplinary lenses of economics, history, literature, philosophy, politics, psychology, and religion. Students learn conceptual tools that support the exercise of leadership in varied settings."[3] This broad, interdisciplinary approach to leadership is practiced in an increasing number of institutions.

Leadership is also conditioned by your role and your organization. For example, as presidential appointees, you are executive leaders, as distinguished from legislative leaders or military leaders. Your role is to serve the president "during the pleasure of the president of the United States for the time being."[4] To carry out this service within the executive branch you will need to attract and motivate followers, use political savvy, use verbal and written communication, develop the skills of others, work with career colleagues, collaborate with formal and informal networks, ensure equity, and promote organizational diversity.

Attracting and Motivating Followers

Perhaps the best way to start examining the relationship between leaders and followers is to determine the objectives of the leader. James MacGregor Burns provides a dichotomy of objectives.[5] Leaders can have both transactional and transformational intentions. It is possible to have an overall transformational purpose but to be acting in a transactional manner at any particular time. The transactional job of the leader is to fill a need that the followers have in such a way that they value the role of the leader. The transformational job of the leader is to elevate the discourse and interactions in such a way that people collectively discover and fulfill their higher-order needs. When they do this, they will value the leadership even more because the leader helps them become more fulfilled than they were before.

Warren Bennis and Burt Nanus talk of motivating people using strategies for generating "attention through vision," "meaning through communication," and "trust through positioning." In each of these strategies they suggest that a leader must fill a deeply held need in the follower, using a vision that "animates, inspirits, [and] transform[s] purpose into action." The leader uses communication in a way that "organizes meaning," so that the tasks and challenges are clear and success is defined as an end state that is difficult to attain but worth the effort. Trust is gained by consistently doing the right things to assure people that the message is genuine.[6]

Even more elemental is the work of Daniel Goleman, who asserts that leadership is "primal." He writes: "The fundamental task of leaders . . . is to prime good feeling in those they lead. That occurs when a leader creates *resonance* [author's emphasis]—a reservoir of positivity that frees the best in people. At root, the primal job of leadership is emotional."[7]

Clearly, presidential appointees must operate on at least two levels simultaneously. First, they must use the political and policy message of the administration to gain the attention of the entire government and external stakeholders; second, they must use their own communication ability to gain the trust of others and the organization as they define the goals of the work and the changes necessary to reach those goals.

Using Political Savvy

The organizational behavior scholar Joel DeLuca has been studying political savvy for more than twenty years. His use of the term is not limited to the political arena but goes beyond:

> While most people are wary of organization politics, politically savvy leaders know how to manage them. They take initiative, and they forge consensus. Ultimately, they help others maximize their impact, so the organization can continue to thrive in a highly competitive future.
>
> Inspirational leadership without a firm grounding in organization politics risks becoming hollow rhetoric. Political savvy discusses how successful leaders at all levels in the organization operate ethically behind the scenes to work the darker side of organizational life.[8]

The emphasis on ethical behavior and behind-the-scenes work is especially crucial in the internal governmental context. As a presidential appointee, you will often have to participate in inter- and intra-agency teams to get things done. Without an understanding of how to take the initiative and forge consensus, it is unlikely that you will be successful in achieving the goals you have set. An example of taking the initiative and forging consensus concerns the Corporation for National and Community Service during the George W. Bush administration. In the midst of major policy change, the corporation was rocked with allegations of mismanagement, and it became necessary to use all of the political savvy of the leaders of the organization to refocus on the mission and demonstrate results. Stephen Goldsmith, chair of the corporation, discussed these challenges with me; see box 4-1.

Using Verbal and Written Communication

Leaders need to foster their verbal and written communications skills. Recognizing the need to do this led to the following assertion: "I wasn't a

BOX 4-1. Applying Political Savvy

Stephen Goldsmith, Chair, Corporation for National and Community Service

After the tumultuous election of 2000 the Bush transition team finally arrived in Washington and began its work. Many issues were high on the list of priorities: tax cuts, faith-based initiatives, defense policies, and more. National service was distinctly not on that list, or anywhere close to it.

AmeriCorps programs—CityYear, Teach for America, and the like—had received high-profile attention from President Clinton. In fact so high that a fair number of Republicans, already anxious about the role of the federal government in local not-for-profit service work, developed strong reservations about the program, then contained in a federal agency called the Corporation for National and Community Service (CNCS).

Yet Governor George Bush in his campaign had spoken of service, and his inaugural speech touched on very consistent themes encouraging Americans to be self-governing citizens, not passive clients of government. Grant recipients and professional staff received some reassurance when President Bush appointed me as chair of CNCS, the parent of AmeriCorps and VISTA. Still, substantial Republican opposition to what they perceived as the liberal and political bias of the corporation threatened its future.

Some professional staff in CNCS, just as in every organization, retained the view that they were guardians of the institutional history against the heretical attacks of a new administration. Others however saw a more constructive future in adapting the institution to the new themes and interests of the incoming administration. The top holdover leadership prepared very thorough briefing books containing descriptions of each program and possible areas of interest. These books however did little to help the new administration understand how it could legitimately incorporate an existing agency into its agenda.

Two possible approaches soon emerged in conversations between me and senior executives. First, CNCS could be much more responsive to faith-based organizations, incorporating them into the fabric of the corporation—not giving them preference but merely being more sensitive to encouraging them to compete and participate. Second, conservatives had criticized CNCS for essentially paying people to be volunteers, a concept to which they objected. Along with staff I began both a programmatic and rhetorical change of the mission of AmeriCorps: those members receiving stipends should be considered the federally paid infrastructure that helps not-for-profit organizations incorporate and utilize true volunteers. The concept of a paid staffer—whether in a local grassroots organization or a campaign—helping train and place volunteers made much more sense to many members. Problematically, though, many of the external stakeholders—programs that received grants and AmeriCorps alums---remained distrustful of the administration and of any shift in emphasis. Senior leadership of the program came around to the new approach, but other stakeholders were slower to show such support.

A new CEO (the corporation equivalent of a cabinet secretary), Les Lenkowsky, did an excellent job of articulating the new policies. The one remaining issue that staff failed to protect against, however, flared up: allegations of mismanagement resulting from complicated accounting questions, which continued to weigh down the organization. However, its emerging new mission helped it survive the resulting management firestorm.

great communicator, but I communicated great things, and they didn't spring full blown from my brow; they came from the heart of a great nation, from our experience, our wisdom, and our belief in the principles that have guided us for two centuries."[9] These words by President Ronald Reagan illustrate the ability of a great communicator to communicate. While demurring about his ability, Reagan linked himself with "the heart of a great nation." What person listening to him did not want to associate with such a heart and with wisdom, belief, and principles?

Former Reagan speech writer Peggy Noonan suggests that a major speech is often the place where policy compromises are made. The fact that the president is about to say something about a particular policy sets a deadline and motivates the various staff factions to find common ground. In a speech, she says, the leader "will tell us who he is and what he wants and how he will get it and what it means that he wants it and what it will mean when he does or does not get it."[10]

As a presidential appointee you will be called upon continually to represent the president, the administration, and your agency in written and verbal communication. The first rule of such communication can be drawn from the medical profession's admonition, "First, do no harm." The appointee must know the rules of the road about who can say what to whom and when. Often the chief of staff or the public affairs director in an agency has outlined specific rules that are available to appointees, particularly about speaking to the press. If such rules are not available, ask the agency's chief of staff what to do about a particular inquiry. If there are interagency implications of a public statement, it may be wise to use the Office of Management and Budget's interagency clearance process.[11] While this process may be somewhat time consuming, it can provide a safe harbor for testimony or major speeches.

Congressional testimony is a unique opportunity for communication. There are restrictions on who may give congressional testimony; often it is limited to those individuals who have been confirmed by the Senate in their current jobs. There are numerous kinds of committees within the legislative branch; a careful analysis of the nature of the committee (such as oversight, authorization, appropriations) is the first step in response to a request to testify.[12] In each case, the request from the committee will specify the nature of the hearing or other setting. Careful review of administration positions, other testimony given on the subject, the membership of the committee, other witnesses who have been invited, and the context in which the hearing is being held are all essential before beginning to prepare testimony.

Typically in formal congressional testimony, two statements are prepared and submitted to the committee in advance once they have gone through the OMB Circular A-19 clearance process. The first is a long statement for the record on the administration's position on the subject. If the administration has not taken a position, it is best to discuss the pros and cons of the issue and not to make policy by yourself. The second document is a statement to be given at the time of the testimony. This should refer to the longer statement and summarize the key points. Both are distributed to the press and the public at the time of the testimony.

Sometimes committees will supply questions in advance. Other times, the ranking and minority members will ask questions—often provided by staff. In either case, your response should be brief and to the point. If you do not know the answer to a question, indicate that you will get back to the committee with the answer.

Following testimony, a copy of the stenographic record will be sent to you for your review. You may revise or clarify points that you made in testimony or in response to questions. Remember that many committees put witnesses under oath, so your final testimony and response to questions should be completely accurate.[13]

Developing the Skills of Others

The tenure of a presidential appointee in a particular position has been established by various studies as between two and three years following confirmation or appointment.[14] This is somewhat misleading, because a particular individual may be called to serve in more than one post over the course of an administration. However, the effect of the short tenure in a single post creates the need for the political appointee to participate in the career development of other individuals in the organization, both political appointees and career civil servants. The need to do so stems from four factors:

—First, there is a need for continuity of policy and operation. Both career and other appointed individuals need to be able to work seamlessly even in the absence of a senior political appointee.

—Second, if policies and operational changes are to be sustained beyond the current administration, career employees need to be able to transfer these policies and changes across administrations. The excellent job that OMB career staff did in sustaining the performance initiatives developed in response to the Government Performance and Results Act demonstrates this fact. Their work served as the basis for performance measurement initiatives in the George W. Bush administration, such as the President's Management Agenda and the program assessment rating tool (PART).

—Third, the career development of specific individuals often depends on the opportunities that senior presidential appointees give them to participate in key decisions and programs.

—Fourth, a strong commitment to training, mentoring, and career development is necessary for the presidential appointee to develop the skills of others. There is a high level of recognition of this need within the intelligence community. The U.S. intelligence community's five-year strategic human capital plan of 2006 highlights three goals for workforce development: to build an agile workforce by projecting and planning for mission-critical human resource requirements; to attract and retain the best and brightest candidates, recognizing and rewarding technical expertise, performance excellence, integrity, and commitment to service; and to create a culture of personal, professional, technical, and managerial leadership at all organizational levels.[15]

Presidential appointees, likewise, have a responsibility to engage in the development of their workforce. The Government Accountability Office says that "designing and implementing . . . human capital systems" is "of critical importance . . . for overall civil service reform."[16] While such systemic transformation is essential at the agency level, the presidential appointee must go beyond this level to the individual level. The Office of Personnel Management provides the following guidance:

—Establish, implement, and evaluate strategic developmental plans that enhance the capacity of employees to meet changing demands.

—Support a learning culture that in turn supports a risk-free exchange of ideas.

—Coach others using goal-defining, feedback, and follow-through approaches to build others' confidence, commitment, skills, and knowledge.

TABLE 4-1. Presidential Appointees' Opinions Regarding Contribution of Their Career Colleagues
Percent

Area of helpfulness	Greatly help	Neutral	Greatly hinder
Technical analysis of difficult issues	91	6	3
Handling day-to-day management tasks	87	11	2
Mastering substantive policy details	87	9	4
Helping with liaison with federal bureaucracy	83	13	4
Anticipating potential policy implementation problems	80	15	5
Helping with liaison with Congress	68	26	7

Source: Judith E. Michaels, *Becoming an Effective Political Executive: 7 Lessons from Former Appointees* (Arlington, Va.: PricewaterhouseCoopers Endowment for the Business of Government, 2001), p. 9.

—Mentor new and younger employees in support of their enculturation, career growth, networking, political savvy, and external awareness.

Working with Career Colleagues

One of the primary differences between public management and private management is personnel constraints. Graham Allison observes that "in government there are two layers of managerial officials that are at times hostile to one another: the civil service (or now the executive system) and the political appointees."[17] This going-in assumption has long plagued political appointees, especially when a change of parties accompanies a change of presidential administrations.

Job one on day one for the presidential appointee should be to lay a foundation for good working relationships with career employees. Presidential scholar Judith Michaels has analyzed interviews and survey information that provide insights into the relationships between "careers" and "politicals." Her observations from the Clinton administration on the perception of appointees regarding the contribution of careerists show that these appointees found their career colleagues invaluable in achieving agency goals (table 4-1).

Although there is no formal prescription for building the relationships between the two groups, some simple suggestions are to respect each other, to treat each other as professionals, to help each other with careers, and to set goals jointly. Dana Michael Harsell has studied the relationships between the two groups in three government agencies and finds that the process of developing the Government Performance and Results Act (GPRA) was beneficial in the following ways:[18]

—The process created a common language for politicals and careerists.

—The process helped smooth the transition in political leadership from the Clinton to the Bush administrations.

—The process required that plans reflect the policy goals of the new administration.

—The process required the setting of ambitious goals.

One of the keys to the long-term success of policies and practices you are seeking to implement will be the degree to which these are institutionalized in the continuing efforts of career staff, who are likely to be there after you are finished with your service. Winning the hearts and minds of careerists is not just about popularity, it is about posterity.

Collaboration

Both formal and informal methods of collaboration are essential to your success as a presidential appointee. In the first case, you should be aware of the formal networks that already exist and get permission to be part of them as quickly as possible. Where no formal networks exist, it may be important for you to create them. But numerous managers have learned, sometimes to their chagrin, that informal or social networks trump formal networks by preventing things from getting done or, if used wisely, by promoting agency objectives. The job of the appointee is to use all of the collaboration tools, inside and outside the agency, to produce results.

As discussed here, collaboration includes five separate functions: managing formal networks, empowering social networks, risk taking, conflict management, and team building.

Managing Formal Networks

The study of networks as tools for management is new, and the principles of "managing in networks and the management of networks" are evolving. An excellent guide to these principles has been developed by Keith

Provan and Brinton Milward.[19] They supply five categories of managing: accountability, legitimacy, conflict, governance, and commitment.

—The management of accountability requires that you determine who is responsible for which outcomes; that you reward compliance with goals; that you monitor your own organization's involvement in the network; that you ensure that dedicated resources are actually used for network activities; and that you ensure that your organization gets credit for its contributions.

—The management of legitimacy requires that you build and maintain the legitimacy of the network's concept, structures, and involvement; that you attract positive publicity; and that you demonstrate the value of network participation.

—The management of conflict requires that you set up mechanisms for conflict resolution; that you act as a good-faith broker; that you make decisions that reflect network goals; that you work to avoid problems with individual members; and that you work inside your own organization to balance its demands with network demands.

—The management of governance requires that you determine which structural governance forms are most appropriate for network success; that you implement and manage these forms; that you recognize when such forms need to change; that you work with other network participants on structure; and that you accept some loss of control over network decisions.

—The management of commitment requires that you are accepted by other participants; that you make sure that other participants understand how the success of the network can contribute to the organization; that you ensure that network resources are used based on network needs; that you build a commitment to network goals; and that you institutionalize your organization's network involvement.

An example of management of networks is the energizing of the Chief Financial Officers Council that occurred in 1993. This network had been established by the Chief Financial Officers Act of 1990. However, it had been dominated by the Office of Management and Budget and was not an effective forum for action until a small group of CFOs met with OMB officials and offered to recharter the organization and create a truly effective means of solving CFO problems. The success of this network led to the creation of others, including the Chief Information Officers Council, the Chief Acquisition Officers Council, and the Chief Human Capital Officers Council.

Empowering Social Networks

One way of looking at social networks is through social network analysis, a formal method for determining the connectedness of various parties. Formal analysis allows the appointee to determine where points of leverage and vulnerability exist and how they might be used or how problems might be addressed. Rob Cross and Andrew Parker propose seven applications for social network analysis:[20]

—Supporting partnerships and alliances by highlighting the effectiveness of information flow, knowledge transfer, and decisionmaking.

—Assessing strategy execution by determining if cross-functional or departmental collaborations support strategic objectives.

—Improving strategic decisionmaking by providing diagnostic information to top leaders.

—Integrating networks across core processes by providing an assessment of the flow of information and knowledge across functions to a core process.

—Promoting innovation by assessing how a team integrates its expertise.

—Ensuring the integration of large-scale change by identifying the change process and the central network people who will sponsor change.

—Developing communities of practice by identifying key members of the community and assessing their connectivity.

The National Academy of Public Administration has recognized the potential of technology-enabled social networks in its Collaboration Project on Web 2.0. An article in *Federal Computer Week* reports that "the Collaboration Project, led by the National Academy of Public Administration, looks to be a center of excellence focused on the Web 2.0 world and how these tools can help government."[21] The goal of the project is to ensure that "leaders who join the Collaboration Project benefit from in-person meetings, virtual forums, and online resources to share best practices, lighthouse cases, white papers, and leadership tools for implementation. All members share a commitment to realizing the promise of Web 2.0 in government."[22] While the Collaboration Project is an example of a community of shared interest, there are other types of networks, such as disaster response and public-private partnerships, that can help the appointee get results.[23]

It is important to remember that networks are only means to the end of producing results that are important to the American people. They are not an end in themselves; at this stage of their development, they are not a replacement for hierarchical relationships.

Risk Taking

Above I speak of getting permission to engage in the work of various collaborative enterprises. This comes under the heading of prudent risk taking. The Peace Corps historically divided its volunteers into three categories: boat rowers, boat rockers, and boat tipperoverers. This distinction is useful to the presidential appointee's approach to taking risk. Everyone is expected to be a boat rower. Crafting and implementing administration policy requires that all be rowing in the same direction. Occasionally, it is necessary to rock the boat.

Senator Lyndon B. Johnson's support of the voting rights bill is the ultimate example of boat rocking. It is described by Taylor Branch in his biography of Martin Luther King: "Majority Leader Lyndon Johnson of Texas worked conspicuously to engineer passage of a bill that would appear more his than Eisenhower's. Careening around the Senate floor often waving his arms in a giant windmill motion to spur the pace of Senate business, Johnson whittled the bill down to minimal form that he thought was the political center of gravity."[24]

Conflict Management

Inevitably, any change (setting goals, making people accountable for their performance, building teams, and so on) produces conflict. You will need to exercise understanding and empathy for the organization and the individuals in it as you analyze the sources of conflict and attempt to resolve it. Inclusiveness and civility are vital for resolving conflicts. Respecting the

LEADING OTHERS **55**

diversity of views and opinions and being willing to make appropriate changes of direction, while reinforcing the goals that have been set, will go a long way toward resolving conflict.

In addition to the commonsense principles outlined above, there are formal techniques available. Perhaps the most famous of these is *Getting to Yes,* by Roger Fisher, William Ury, and Bruce Patton of the Harvard Negotiation Project. They have applied their techniques to negotiations as well as resolution of seemingly intractable conflicts. Their principles are simple:[25]

—Don't bargain over positions.

—Separate people from the problem.

—Focus on interests not positions.

—Invent options for mutual gain.

—Insist on using objective criteria.

Using these principles to analyze and defuse conflict is a skill that can be learned. Again, as with team building, there are training programs available to help.[26] Charles Field, a teacher at the University of Maryland School of Public Policy and a frequent lecturer on negotiation techniques, supplies an example from Zaire of how the techniques can be applied.

Following the genocide involving Hutu and Tutsi ethnic groups—in which over 300,000 lives were lost—a peace treaty was brokered that entailed power sharing between these two groups. Seemingly insurmountable barriers of mistrust and fractured communication separated the two communities, and there was significant doubt as to whether implementation of the peace agreement would succeed.

The Wilson Center for International Scholars . . . was invited in 2003 to work with the parties to develop a leadership program that would enable them to shift from zero-sum thinking to a recognition of interdependence and common interests; to establish trust between leaders; to strengthen collaboration skills; and to rebuild a consensus about the rules of the game. At the heart of this leadership training were principles of interest-based negotiation.

Key leaders from all sectors of Burundi society have taken this training and have forged working relationships that now allow them to confront problems not as enemies but as joint problem solvers. They have used these skills to reach effective integration of the army and the police. Political leaders have used these skills to help them reach consensus on the conduct of national elections.[27]

Team Building

John Donne says, "No man is an island entire and unto himself." These words are probably most apt for leaders. Our earlier definition of leadership is, "Leadership is the process by which one individual influences others to accomplish desired goals."[28] The "others" often constitute a team of disparate individuals who must work toward a common purpose. The first rule of leadership, also noted above, is that leaders must have followers. These followers must also work together in harmonious ways to promote the objectives of the organization.

Rosabeth Moss Kanter looks at team building and the role that instilling confidence plays in creating winning teams:

> The three cornerstones of that foundation [of team confidence] are accountability, collaboration, and initiative. Accountability means you've examined the facts and your own abilities; you've worked hard to improve your abilities so you know you can take responsibility in a given situation and be accountable for performance. Collaboration means that you support and are supported by the people around you. And initiative translates to an action you can take with the sense that you're in control of it.[29]

Accountability, collaboration, and initiative—concepts for the leader to keep in mind for building high-performing teams. Often the role of the leader must include coaching and mentoring and continually reinforcing the importance of each person's role to the team. Peter Drucker reminds us that "teams are tools."[30] The job of the presidential appointee is to create a strong but flexible team that can use its diversity to create and implement the policies of the president. There are many techniques for doing this, and learning them and using them will help you achieve the goals you have set for yourself and your agency.[31]

Ensuring Equity

The history of the public administration movement often highlights the roles of economy, efficiency, and effectiveness in producing what the British call value for money. There is, however, a fourth *e*, and that is equity.[32] In any list of governmental achievements, the concept of equity and fairness will be present. In business it may be a good practice to promote equity and organizational diversity. In a public setting, it is the key to organizational success. The public administration scholar George Frederickson quotes from Woodrow Wilson's seminal essay on public administration to support the fundamental nature of equity for the public administrator: "The ideal for us is a civil service cultured and self-sufficient enough to act with sense and vigor, and yet so intimately connected with the popular thought, by means of elections and constant public counsel, as to find arbitrariness or class spirit quite out of the question."[33]

In the development of policy, affirmative efforts need to be made to ensure that the inequities that plague our society are forthrightly addressed. Concepts such as environmental justice, equal treatment before the law, and decent housing for all are examples of the programmatic imperatives that the presidential appointee faces. Knowledge of the law of the land, especially as reviewed by the Supreme Court, is an unassailable starting place for public leaders. Below is a list of antidiscrimination laws passed since 1963:

—1963, Equal Pay Act
—1964, Civil Rights Act
—1967, Age Discrimination in Employment Act
—1978, Civil Service Reform Act
—1990, Americans with Disabilities Act
—1991, Civil Rights Act of 1991

Several concepts of equity are of particular interest to the presidential appointee. The first is fairness. Is the process of access to government fair to all members of the public? Is inclusion routinely practiced when developing regulations? Are individuals or groups disadvantaged by the government's action? These kinds of questions go to the heart of public administration. Process fairness must be taken into account by appointees for several reasons: first, it is the right thing to do; second, it is required by law and regulation; finally, failure to follow appropriate processes can result in Congress or the courts overturning executive policy.

While ensuring a fair process is important, it is not a goal in itself. Equitable distribution of government program benefits is as important, if not more important, than process fairness. This equity of result must be continually evaluated after the fact to determine if good intentions and good processes produced the desired results. For example, are programs that are designed to ensure fairness in housing actually promoting that fairness? Or are they simply moving the problem from one location to another? The answer to this question should be determined through careful evaluation of various efforts around the country. For example, a similar question arises in regard to the location of facilities designed to contain or eliminate hazardous materials. How do we decide where superfund cleanups should be undertaken? How was the Yucca Mountain site chosen for the disposal of nuclear waste?

Beyond the legal requirements for diversity, which are often met under the concept of fairness, a more important argument for organizational diversity can be made on principles similar to those of biodiversity, which are now widely accepted. An organization that has an overwhelming predominance of a single racial, ethnic, or gender group is susceptible to "group think" and is unlikely to respond in a nuanced way to complex problems. Not including multiple points of view within the organization can lead to both policy and implementation failures stemming from an inability to fully understand a problem, to mobilize a guiding coalition, or to achieve the results that people want.

One example of harm to an organization stemming from a failure to resolve the problems of institutional diversity is the "Don't ask, don't tell" military policy established in 1993, at the beginning of the Clinton administration. Under this compromise, gays cannot serve openly in the military. The policy not only inflicted a great deal of political harm on Clinton early in his first term but also caused serious difficulties for the Pentagon. Mark Thompson notes the following:

> About 12,000 service members have been booted from the military since the law took effect, including dozens of Arabic speakers whose skills are particularly prized by the military since the advent of the war on terror. While the number discharged for their sexuality has fallen from 1,273 in 2001 to 612 in 2006, Pentagon officials insist they are applying the law as fairly as ever. Gay rights advocates disagree, suggesting that the military—pressed for personnel amid an unpopular war—is willing to ignore sexual orientation when recruiting becomes more difficult. Last May, a CNN poll found that 79 percent of Americans feel that homosexuals should be allowed to serve in the military.[34]

Social equity, as it applies to public administration, is defined by the National Academy of Public Administration Social Equity panel as "the fair, just, and equitable management of all institutions serving the public directly or by contract; and the fair, just, and equitable distribution of public services, implementation of public policy, and commitment to promote fairness, justice, and equity in the formation of public policy."[35] The panel also lists the following:

—Procedural fairness: Provide due process, equal protection, and equal rights to all persons regardless of their personal characteristics. Each individual should be treated fairly, and any instances of unfair treatment of individuals should be corrected. Furthermore, existing and new practices in implementation, service delivery, and management should be examined to ensure that procedural fairness is not disproportionately denied to any group of persons.

—Distribution and access: Distribute services and benefits equally or in such a way that those who are less advantaged receive greater benefits. This general principle should guide the observance of requirements that are multiple and complex and that vary with the purpose of a program or the problem that is being addressed. For existing policies and programs, distribution and access should match the intended purpose.

—Quality: Ensure that there is consistency in the quality of services and benefits delivered to all groups of people. Although some persons have the means to secure enhanced quality, public administrators should strive to ensure that prevailing standards of acceptable practice are met for all groups.

—Outcomes: Seek to achieve an equal level of accomplishment or outcome in the social and economic conditions for all individuals and seek to eliminate differences in outcomes or groups.

—Related responsibilities: Guarantee all a place at the table so that they can express their own views about public policy choices and service delivery. Take proactive and affirmative efforts to involve all citizens and solicit feedback.

Promoting Organizational Diversity

A related area of importance is the development of an organization's culture. A culture that is one-dimensional because of an unwillingness or inability to promote diversity of opinion needs to open up a discussion of the issues it faces. An example of a problem stemming from a lack of diversity in culture is contained in the report on the investigation into the crash of the space shuttle *Columbia*.[36] The following excerpt highlights the effects of the failure of leaders to build resilient teams capable of overcoming the cultural biases that occur within organizations.

> The Board recognized early on that the accident was probably not an anomalous, random event, but rather likely rooted to some degree in NASA's history and the human space flight program's culture. Accordingly, the Board broadened its mandate at the outset to include an investigation of a wide range of historical and organizational issues, including political and budgetary considerations, compromises, and changing priorities over the life of the space shuttle program. The Board's conviction regarding the importance of these factors strengthened as the investigation progressed, with the result that this report, in its findings, conclusions, and recommendations, places as much weight on these causal factors as on the more easily understood and corrected physical cause of the accident.
>
> The organizational causes of this accident are rooted in the space shuttle program's history and culture, including the original compromises that were required to gain approval for the shuttle, subsequent years of resource constraints, fluctuating priorities, schedule pressures, mischaracterization of the shuttle as operational rather than developmental, and lack of an agreed national vision for human space flight. Cultural traits and organizational practices detrimental to safety were allowed to develop, including reliance on past success as a substitute for sound engineering practices; . . . organizational barriers that prevented effective communication of critical safety information and stifled professional differences of opinion; lack of integrated management across program elements; and the evolution of an informal chain of command and decisionmaking processes that operated outside the organization's rules.

One way to mitigate problems of cultural narrowness is to promote organizational diversity. Scott Page concludes that diversity in an organization can be more important than individual ability in solving problems: "Individuals can accomplish only so much. We are limited in our abilities.

Our heads contain only so many neurons and axons. Collectively, we face no such constraint. We possess incredible capacity to think differently. These differences can provide the seeds of innovation, progress, and understanding."[37]

Page distinguishes between identity diversity (who we are) and cognitive diversity (how and what we think) and suggests that both are important, especially given the globalization of organizations and the move to diverse teams. On the cognitive side, Page posits four frameworks for promoting diversity:

—Perspectives: ways of representing situations and problems.

—Interpretations: ways of categorizing or partitioning perspectives.

—Heuristics: ways of generating solutions to problems.

—Predictive models: ways of inferring cause and effect.

Taking into account these four frameworks while at the same time promoting identity diversity will have the dual benefit of enhancing equity within the organization and avoiding cultural bias.

FIVE

Leading Yourself

"**K**now thyself" is an adage as old as Greek mythology. It is variously attributed to Socrates, Thales, and Pythagoras, among others. Often when we see it, we tend to move on and think, "Right. Got that one." But do we? The nine attributes discussed below can serve as a checklist for these questions with regard to yourself as a presidential appointee. What is your motivation for public service? Do you have self-awareness, honesty, integrity, courage? Are you a life-long learner? Are you skilled at trusting and at gaining trust? Are you confident, decisive, and resilient? Are you empathetic, a good listener? And not least, are you emotionally intelligent?

Public Service Motivation

"Public service," according to former comptroller general Elmer Staats, "is a concept, an attitude, a sense of duty—yes, even a sense of public morality."[1] Staats sets a high bar for the rest of us, even though the notion of public service as a moral necessity may have been taught to us since childhood. Plato makes it a bit more practical: "The price good men pay for indifference to public affairs is to be ruled by evil men." Whatever the wording, motivation for public service is essential to being effective in the role of presidential appointee. Further, you probably would not be reading this if you did not have some form of public service motivation. Other observers may be more cynical: John Gardner, the former secretary of health, education, and welfare and founder of Common Cause, says, "So now we have a new Administration. The venal and obsequious gather round. But fortunately, so do some very able people. And sometimes, of course, they are indistinguishable."[2]

Your job as a new presidential appointee is to distinguish yourself as one of the "very able people," free from the venality and obsequiousness that Gardner describes and, moreover, following the "sense of duty" that Staats speaks of. One scholar—Indiana University professor James Perry—who has done extensive research in measuring public service motivation says, "Public service motivation . . . represents an individual's predisposition to respond to motives grounded primarily or uniquely in public institutions. The construct is associated conceptually with six dimensions: attraction to public policymaking, commitment to the public interest, civic duty, social justice, self-sacrifice, and compassion."[3]

In general, highly effective public leaders have these six dimensions. They may manifest themselves in different ways depending on different philosophies of government. Certainly Ronald Reagan and his administration took a different approach from that of Bill Clinton and his administration, yet a sense of pursuing the public good pervaded both. This abstract notion has to be translated into concrete action. The Office of Personnel Management competency framework summarizes these actions as follows: "Shows a commitment to serve the public. Ensures that actions meet public needs. Aligns organizational objectives and practices with public interests."[4]

The concept of stewardship expands the personal dimension to a general understanding of what the public needs and how an organization can fill that need. As used in government, the concept of stewardship represents a fundamental respect for the public good and also the means used to achieve it. This respect can find a more concrete form in the concept of public value. Although steeped in ancient tradition, a more recent formulation comes from Harvard professor Mark Moore, who suggests that public value is defined not only by the customers of government but also by the public, as it participates in the process of electing and financially supporting government.[5]

This idea adds an additional dimension to public service. Perhaps it is best expressed in my own modification of Robert Kaplan's notion of the balanced scorecard for the public sector (chapter 1). Results must be produced efficiently to ensure public support, but these results must meet the needs of customers and inspire the confidence of the public. All of these efforts must be undertaken simultaneously, guided by the vision of the president and the agency head. Public service motivation requires that leaders understand what the public is demanding and produce it in a way that meets this demand in the most efficient, effective, economical, and equitable way possible. This activity is not limited to the executive branch. The concept of stewardship is spelled out in the *Performance and Accountability Report* of the Government Accountability Office (an arm of Congress): "The Congress needs information to make sound judgments that will benefit this nation in the short term and over the long run. Thus to further assist our client with its oversight function and aid its insight and foresight, we revised our list of federal programs and areas at risk of fraud, waste, abuse, and mismanagement and in need of broad-based transformation."[6]

Oversight, insight, and foresight became the watchwords at the Government Accountability Office (GAO) under the leadership of former comptroller general David Walker. These three concepts provide a good guide for presidential appointees as stewards of the public. Oversight reflects critical thinking—stewardship that steers programs and policies. Insight is the ability to see into the core of issues and find ways to solve problems before they create roadblocks. Foresight is the ability to foresee the long-run implications of current actions.

A particular example of foresight is the work of Walker and the GAO in examining the fiscal future of the nation. The objective of this work is "to state the facts and speak the truth regarding the nation's current financial condition and long-term fiscal outlook in order to increase public awareness and accelerate actions by appropriate federal, state, and local officials."[7] For you as a presidential appointee, the implications of GAO's projections are significant and vital to understand. The National Academy of Public Administration realizes that "there are no easy solutions to the mismatch between what the American people expect from government

and how much they are willing to pay. Policymakers and the public must
. . . confront the difficult trade-offs that are required to restore sustainable
fiscal policy."[8]

The reason most people accept an appointment to work in the federal
government is to get something done or to make a difference. While the
definition of these terms will vary from administration to administration,
the presidential appointee should have an orientation toward accom-
plishing the objectives of the president and the administration. It is sometimes necessary to look back at prior administrations to get a view of what
might be possible. Noted author Paul Light's list of the twenty-five major
government accomplishments over the last five decades can serve as a
guide as to what might be possible (see box 5-1).

Self-Awareness

Another key ingredient of leadership of self is the ability to win others over
to your ideas and initiatives.[9] This has been referred to as the art of woo.
Richard Shell and Mario Moussa, the main prophets of wooing, define it
as follows: "So what is Woo? It is relationship-based persuasion, a strategic process for getting people's attention, pitching your ideas, and obtaining approval for your plans and projects. It is in short one of the most
important skills in the repertoire of an entrepreneur, employee, or professional manager whose work requires them to rely on influence and persuasion rather than coercion and force."[10]

Shell and Moussa present five styles of woo across two dimensions. The
dimensions are volume and orientation. Next time you are in a meeting
with a group of peers, listen to the volume of each person's presentation.
Are they loud and strident or quiet and contained? Or are they somewhere
in between? Which approach seems to be working? Do individuals seem
to be able to modulate their tone in response to the attitudes of those they
are seeking to influence? In your own interactions what is your volume
and do you adjust it to meet the situation? Maybe consciously adjusting
your own volume, up or down, could help you become more effective.

On the second dimension, are you primarily self-oriented or other-
oriented? In some cases, self-orientation seems most appropriate. Secretary

BOX 5-1. **Government's Greatest Achievements: From Civil Rights to Homeland Defense**

—Rebuilding Europe after World War II
—Expanding the right to vote
—Promoting equal access to public accommodations
—Reducing disease
—Reducing workplace discrimination
—Ensuring safe food and drinking water
—Strengthening the nation's highway system
—Increasing health care access for older Americans
—Reducing the federal budget deficit
—Promoting financial security in retirement
—Improving water quality
—Supporting veterans' readjustment and training
—Promoting scientific and technological research
—Containing communism
—Improving air quality
—Enhancing workplace safety
—Strengthening the national defense
—Reducing hunger and improve nutrition
—Increasing access to postsecondary education
—Enhancing consumer protection
—Expanding foreign markets for U.S. goods
—Increasing the stability of financial institutions and markets
—Increasing arms control and disarmament
—Protecting the wilderness
—Promoting space exploration

Source: Paul Light, *Government's Greatest Achievements: From Civil Rights to Homeland Defense* (Brookings, 2002), p. 62.

of State Alexander Haig certainly felt that way when he famously announced "I am in control here" after the assassination attempt on Ronald Reagan. Unfortunately for Haig, his assertion was overly self-oriented, and his understanding of the constitutional line of succession was erroneous. Other-oriented individuals will seek the audience's viewpoint and mold their presentations to the interests of the group they are addressing. But before we too quickly conclude that one technique is better than another, we should consider that both have downsides. In his book *The Lonely Crowd,* David Riesman suggests that overreliance on other-directed social orientation could lead to dysfunctional conformity.[11] The key skill is to find a balance that is true to your inner principles while fine-tuning your argument to the audience.

The five styles of wooing are similar to the typology created by the psychoanalyst Carl Jung and refined by the psychological theorist Isabel Briggs. According to Jung's and Briggs's typology, all people can be classified using the following four paired sets of criteria: extraversion/introversion, sensing/intuition, thinking/feeling, and judging/perceiving. From these the Myers-Briggs type indicator was developed.[12]

—Extroversion/introversion defines a person's source and direction of energy. The extrovert's source and direction are mainly in the external world. The introvert's source and direction are mainly in the internal world.

—Sensing/intuition defines a person's method of perceiving information. Sensing means that a person believes mainly information he or she receives directly from the external world. Intuition means that a person believes mainly information he or she receives from the internal or imaginative world.

—Thinking/feeling defines how a person processes information. Thinking means that a person makes a decision mainly through logic. Feeling means that a person makes a decision based on emotion.

—Judging/perceiving defines how a person implements the information he or she has processed. Judging means that a person organizes and acts on life events according to preconceived plans. Perceiving means that the person improvises and seeks alternatives.

You can use the Myers-Briggs type indicator yourself, both as an individual guide and as a guide in your organization. It should be used, of course, as only one element of judging self-awareness. And you should remember that there are no right answers in these pairings: they are simply a way for you to get to know yourself better and, in doing so, to recognize both your strengths and those of others, whose insights can augment and complement your own. Unfortunately, there is a human tendency to overestimate the importance of one's own strengths and denigrate those who have the strengths we lack. This can result in assuming that those who differ from us are wrong—rather than just that they view the situation through a different lens. The more that we know about our own preferences and nonpreferences, the easier it is to appreciate the preferences of others.

The noted author—and the director of the James MacGregor Burns Academy of Leadership—Carol Pearson can take you in a similar direction. Her book *Awakening the Heroes Within* provides a practical spiritual journey in personal leadership. "Heroism is also not just about finding a new truth but about having the courage to act on that vision. That is, in a very practical way, why heroes need to have the courage and care associated with strong ego development and the vision and clarity of mind and spirit that come from having taken their souls' journey and gain the treasure of their true selves."[13]

As a new presidential appointee, you have embarked on a life journey that will likely be both compelling and brief in terms of your overall life. Knowing yourself as you prepare for the journey, embark on it, and return from it will be essential to your effectiveness while in the job and your future afterward.

Honesty and Integrity

Every administration provides admonitions similar to that of White House Chief of Staff Andy Card's comments to presidential appointees: "Recognize that working in this administration means that you should have the courage to follow the rules, obviously, and stay within the law, obviously. But it's actually to do more than that. Recognize that you do have a moral compass that tells you what to do and to do the right thing, and we'd like to see everyone do the right thing."[14] The idea of the moral compass is an important one. While the Office of Government Ethics is the umpire on ethics issues, there needs to be a coach in each agency and every office.[15] Presidential appointees can exercise great leadership on this issue in two ways. First, through their own actions they should demonstrate that they take these issues seriously and insist that their appointed and civil service colleagues do the same. Second, they can periodically convene groups to discuss the issues. There are numerous tools inside and outside of government that deal not only with the rules and laws but also with the grey areas of ethical behavior.

No presidential administration in the history of the United States has been free from scandal and allegations of scandal. The lesson many learned, certainly from Watergate and beyond, is that often it is not the deed but the cover-up that is the most devastating part of an incident. Telling the truth to the appropriate official as quickly as possible is the best way to avoid the tragedy of guilt by association with a malfeasance. The subject of political scandals is sufficiently ubiquitous that two websites present lists of major scandals in federal, state, and local government.[16] These range from bribery to hiring illegal aliens for domestic work. The best advice we can give to presidential appointees is to consult their general counsel before taking a questionable action and to be sure not to do anything that they would not want printed in the *Washington Post*.

You may have been asked the following question at vetting: "Have you ever done anything that would embarrass the president?" Keeping this standard in mind as you serve as an appointee may prevent behavior that will cause difficulties.

Courage

Some leadership scholars have called courage the Wallenda factor.[17] Warren Bennis and Burt Nanus assert that great leaders do not even think about failure. They have an ability to focus on success, and like the great tightrope walker Karl Wallenda, they put all of their energies into their task and none into visualizing what failure looks like. Harry Truman once said, "Whenever I make a bum decision, I just go out and make another one." This institutional and intestinal courage to keep pressing on in the face of adversity, even self-inflicted adversity, is a hallmark of the successful presidential appointee.

Very often, there will be a crisis that needs rapid and resolute action. The buck stops with the political appointee in charge, and he or she must have the courage to act quickly to solve the problem and also to protect the president or the presidency. While this may sound melodramatic, read the archives of the *New York Times* and see how often the failure to take rapid effective action has harmed an administration. The Katrina disaster comes to mind, but it is only one example.

Public management scholar Don Kettl describes the arrival in New Orleans of Admiral Thad Allen, who is now the commandant of the Coast Guard:

> As [Admiral Allen] arrived in New Orleans, a small helicopter carrier had tied up at the dock. It was one of the few places in the city with reliable communication, electric power, a dry place to sleep, air conditioning, and hot food. He brought in the parish's emergency services commander and asked him what he needed. The response was simple. "Hope," he said. Allen choked back his emotions and set to work supplying just that. He became coordinator-in-chief of the government's recovery operations, and things began happening. He did not manage by command, although with his military position, presidential charge, and bulldog-like demeanor he could have done just that. Rather, he worked hard to establish partnerships among the players: to define the mission that had to be [undertaken], to identify the contributions of each organization to that mission, and to motivate everyone to contribute their part. That approach quickly began to pay off; it was how . . . things got done. . . . Allen later called this a focus on unity of effort instead of unity of command. Results, not control, mattered most. He built partnerships on the results the region needed, and results were what he got.[18]

Lifelong Learning

The Office of Personnel Management says that the lifelong learner
—Grasps the essence of new information.
—Masters new technical and business knowledge.
—Recognizes own strengths and weaknesses.
—Pursues self-development.
—Seeks feedback from others and opportunities to master new knowledge.[19]

Whether this is called lifelong or continual learning, the idea is the same: we must process new information constantly and adapt our behavior accordingly. This is not the same as being unprincipled. Both the individual and the organization must continually learn and adapt to new challenges within the context of the moral and policy frameworks that they embrace.

Peter Senge expresses the nature of learning as follows:

Real learning gets to the heart of what it means to be human. Through learning we re-create ourselves. Through learning we become able to do something we were never able to do. Through learning we reperceive the world and our relationship to it. Through learning we extend our capacity to create, to be part of the generative process of life. There is within each of us a deep hunger for this type of learning.[20]

Senge and others extend this sense of learning to organizations; such learning organizations are continually able to adapt, to visualize, and to create their own futures. In the case of public organizations, they must be led by individuals who are capable of learning in their own right, so they can create an environment in which the organization has the capacity to change positively in response to external change, whether it be demographic, scientific, economic, international relations, or policy.

Presidential appointees in the Department of the Interior exhibited this kind of learning in their approach to dealing with environmental challenges in 2001, when Gail Norton was confirmed as George W. Bush's secretary of the department. According to Stephen Goldsmith and Bill Eggers,

Norton and her leadership team . . . discovered that . . . the physical landscape had . . . altered dramatically [over the past few decades]. Developers were chopping large properties into small parcels. Cities and suburbs were sprawling across the previously wide-open West, where once, in the course of an hour, you might have seen one cowboy and a few cows. . . .

The new leadership . . . believed the department needed fresh tools based on a spirit of collaboration and local knowledge. . . . They needed new strategies for managing land use. And they needed to stop looking inward and start looking outward. . . .

Instead of dictating policy from on high [the new leadership] worked with state and local officials and landowners to figure out how they could utilize land while protecting natural resources.

The new environmentalism they outlined focused on local ideas, incentives, and innovation. The goal: to create a context in which companies, organizations, and individuals were inspired to become citizen stewards, and where people make decisions in an integrated fashion.[21]

Trusting and Gaining Trust

Bennis and Nanus have an apt epigram for trust: the "lubrication" that causes organizations to work: "Trust requires accountability, predictability, and reliability."[22]

The first aspect of trust, accountability, comes from setting goals and putting together the means to reach them. The setting of goals can be very frightening to the public leader, who might ask, What if I set a goal and fail? What if failure wasn't my fault? How can I set a goal if I have to rely on others or circumstances beyond my control to reach it? Can I really be held responsible for outcomes? If I fail will failure reflect badly on the president? The answer, of course, is to ignore such fear and to set bold goals.

A government example of a bold goal is President John F. Kennedy's call for a program to put a man on the moon within the decade. "We choose to go to the moon," he said and followed with, "We choose to go to the moon in this decade." And gave his reasons: "Not because [it is] easy, but because [it is] hard, because that goal will serve to organize and measure the best of our energies and skills, because that challenge is one that we are willing to accept, one we are unwilling to postpone, and one that we intend to win."[23]

Kennedy entrusted the presidential appointee James Webb, the second administrator of NASA, to get the job done. Webb in turn organized a cadre of federal civil servants, scientists, and people from the private sector. He earned their trust and instilled in them the courage to accomplish what many felt was impossible.

The second aspect of trust, predictability, means giving the same answer every time a question is asked regardless of who asks it or how the question is framed. If a goal is clear and communicated well, it will become predictable. Treasury Secretary Paul O'Neill set a goal of finalizing the *Financial Report of the United States Government* soon after the end of the fiscal year. Before this the financial statement had often taken more than six months to complete. However, the goal was predictable and clear. It was met in late 2004 just after O'Neill's tenure as secretary of the Treasury came to an end.

The third aspect of trust, reliability, is the personal dimension associated with predictability. If the financial report was to get done on time, the staff at Treasury had to be able to rely on O'Neill not to change his mind. They had to use the secretary's mandate to organize agencies across the government as well as within Treasury. As Steve App, CFO at Treasury at the time, said, "Once Secretary O'Neill clearly laid out this challenge, he was steadfast in both his interest and support in achieving it, commenting (in writing to me) on our monthly progress reports, and personally attending key agency meetings where I needed his presence to motivate any remaining skeptics. Such leadership on his part was crucial to us successfully achieving the goal."[24]

Confidence, Decisiveness, and Resilience

The leadership scholar Rosabeth Moss Kanter makes a strong distinction between the self-confidence of a leader and the ability to instill confidence in an organization or inspire others to have confidence in the organization:

> But we haven't made the connection between that broad sense of whether people have confidence in their leader and the self-confidence of the leader. So I set about to understand this linkage, and what I discovered is that while many leaders have self-confidence, the most important thing is whether they have confidence in *other* people and therefore create the conditions in which the people they lead can get the work done.[25]

Not only must leaders have enough confidence in themselves to undertake the kind of ambitious objectives listed above and to reject the conceptualization of failure, they must also build the confidence of others, both inside and outside the organization. As Kanter says, "Leadership is not about the leader; it is about how the leader builds the confidence of everyone else. Leaders deliver confidence by espousing high standards in their messages, exemplifying these standards in the conduct they model, and establishing formal mechanisms to provide a structure for acting on those standards."[26]

Elsewhere we quote Harry Truman saying, "Whenever I make a bum decision, I go out and make another one." This kind of resilience enabled him to withstand the firestorm of criticism he received after firing General Douglas MacArthur. The cause of the firing was MacArthur's view on expansion of the war in Korea and carrying the fight into China. Truman feared that such an action would provoke the Soviet Union and result in World War III. Once the decision to fire MacArthur was made, Truman never looked back despite the political theater of MacArthur's "Old Soldiers Never Die" speech before Congress. Having the courage to act, the decisiveness to act quickly, and the resilience to withstand the criticism that comes from sticking to your guns are personal characteristics that presidential appointees need to cultivate.

Empathy and Good Listening

Advice from Stephen Covey, the author of *The 7 Habits of Highly Effective People*, is to "seek first to understand and then to be understood."[27] Empathy, the ability to understand, can be both intellectual and emotional. The best empathy has both characteristics; showing people you understand their point of view and how they feel helps them trust and have confidence in you.

One way to develop empathy is to practice the very difficult art of listening. We put ourselves in the place of the other person and seek not to frame our reply but to understand the source of the other individual's communication. If done right, this practice allows us to understand, at a fundamental level, the fears, aspirations, and intentions of the speaker. This understanding can help us develop the leader-follower relationship necessary to leading others.

Covey warns us that empathetic listening is risky. It takes a great deal of security to go into a deep listening experience because you open yourself up to being influenced. You become vulnerable. In order to have influence, you must be influenced. This requires courage. An example of empathetic listening is that of Robert Reich, secretary of labor in the Clinton administration. Some weeks after his appointment as labor secretary Reich held a meeting of employees and asked for ideas. Steve Wandner, a career employee, suggested that laid-off workers who file for unemployment insurance be screened to determine the cause of their job loss (and if the cause were fundamental to the industry, that the worker be immediately eligible for retraining and job placement help). Despite its novelty, Wandner's idea later became part of the unemployment regulations.[28]

Emotional Intelligence

Daniel Goleman and his colleagues suggest that "great leadership works through emotions. No matter what leaders set out to do—whether it's creating strategy or mobilizing teams to action—their success depends on how they do it. Even if they get everything else just right, if leaders fail at the primal task of driving emotions in the right direction, nothing they do will work as well as it could or should."[29] Goleman divides emotional intelligence into personal capabilities and social capabilities.[30] Under personal capabilities he lists self-awareness and self-management; under social capabilities he lists social awareness and relationship management.

—Self-awareness includes emotional self-awareness, accurate self-assessment, and self-confidence.

—Self-management includes emotional self-control, transparency, adaptability, achievement, initiative, and optimism.

—Social awareness includes empathy, organizational awareness, and service.

—Relationship management includes being an inspiration and a catalyst for change, having influence, developing others, managing conflict, and collaborating.

Goleman's framework demonstrates that leaders need to consciously take control of their emotions. Public leaders often guide not just their organizations but the public perception of those organizations. Self-management allows leaders to inspire public confidence in the process by which goals are achieved as well as in the goals themselves. Often, managers are seen as technocrats, with no understanding of human nature. As a presidential appointee, you should undertake the antithesis of the technocratic approach. While you should possess the requisite technical knowledge and skills, your orientation should be toward using your entire persona to help solve the problems of the nation.

SIX

Maintaining
Global Awareness

"Think globally. Act locally." This adage is used by many groups to advise their members how to behave. The same is true for presidential appointees. First, they must exhibit external awareness at home. Then they must look around the world at the trends that will affect them and seek opportunities to use these trends, positive and negative, in carrying out their assignments. Beyond that, they must reach out and connect appropriate global partners and customers with the federal government. While not every agency will have programs with global impacts, all agencies are certain to be impacted by global trends.

Mary Ellen Joyce, the director of executive development programs at the Brookings Institution, points out five general behavioral characteristics associated with having a global mindset:[1]

—Recognizes impact of globalization on business or organization.

—Makes decisions incorporating global considerations.

—Helps others understand the impacts of globalization.

—Understands global geography and politics.

—Learns from other countries and cultures.

These characteristics presuppose an external awareness on the part of the leader or manager. The description of this competency includes overall external awareness and extends it to the potential effect that events and trends beyond the United States will have on your work as a presidential appointee.

External Awareness

The Office of Personnel Management defines external awareness in terms of the successful organization's ability to scan its environment as part of a strategic planning process. Environmental scanning is seen as an essential approach to problem solving in the complex environment of the twenty-first century. This is true of scans on all levels: locally, nationally, and most of all globally.

This dual importance of global awareness and environmental scanning is especially notable in work for the federal government. Scholar Don Kettl observes that an environmental scan of the issues that federal officials had to deal with after the 9/11 terrorist attacks involved core questions about the nature of government: "In globalization, important changes occurred: the fall of communism, America's rise as the world's unchallenged military power, the growing importance of global economic markets, and the unexpected challenge of global terror networks. Americans found themselves, for the first time ever, struggling to redefine the boundaries of federalism, privatization, and globalization."[2] Kettl's observation aptly describes the task before the presidential appointee. He or she must continually examine global threats and be ready to design new responses for them.

Julie Gerberding, director of the Centers for Disease Control and Prevention, is in a special position to recognize the importance of organizational and programmatic responses to global threats:

> When the SARS outbreak started . . . a doctor in the Guangdong Province of China . . . taking care of SARS patients . . . actually was coming down with the virus. . . . He went to Hong Kong to visit his brother and stayed at a hotel with many others. . . . Within a 48-hour period, hotel visitors [who had] picked up the virus . . . transfused it to every corner of the world. There is nothing that illustrates better, I believe, the incredible speed, connectivity, and globalization of our contemporary world. Something that started out in a remote corner of the Guangdong Province became a global health crisis . . . in a matter of days.[3]

In the global fight against SARS and other diseases, individuals and groups from around the world feed data into centralized computer systems managed by the CDC. This system is constructed as a network that rigorously assigns roles, thus protecting privacy and confidentiality of data while at the same time providing vital information to those with a need to know.

While you may not be confronted with anything as threatening as a SARS epidemic, the need to be continually aware of the external environment and global trends remains. Your job will be to design solutions—networked and otherwise—to meet global opportunities and threats.

Technology and Globalization

The writer Thomas Friedman talked to the journalist Ted Koppel about the changes in technology that are fostering the increasing pace of globalization that confronts the presidential appointee. He suggested that the convergence of the personal computer (which allows individuals to become authors of their own content in digital form), the Internet and the World Wide Web, and interoperable software spurred a "global platform" for collaboration. Friedman noted the effects of this convergence as follows: "So when I say that the world is flat I'm not suggesting the world is equal, that suddenly we're all equal. What I am saying, though, is that more people today than ever before have access to a technology platform for innovation, entrepreneurship, education—and unfortunately, Ted, also for terrorism—than ever before. That's what I mean."[4]

An example of the government's lack of preparedness for this technological shift was the problems encountered by the State Department following the embassy bombings in Dar es Salaam, Tanzania, and Nairobi, Kenya, by al Qaeda. At that time, the State Department was heavily criticized for the inadequate technology connecting its embassies and missions around the world. According to a 1999 report of the Overseas Presence Advisory Panel, "We were dismayed to find that our embassies are equipped with antiquated, grossly inefficient, and incompatible information technology systems incapable of even the simplest electronic communications across department lines."[5] To remedy this finding, the panel recommended the president to "direct all overseas agencies to immediately provide all overseas staff with Internet access, e-mail, a secure unclassified Internet website, and shared applications permitting unclassified communications among all agencies and around the globe. Furthermore, agencies should initiate planning for a common platform for secure classified information to be implemented over the next two years."

Criticism like this has led to reform in information sharing in the State Department and also across the foreign affairs community. However, a new presidential appointee would be wise to test and evaluate the ability of his or her agency to communicate in an interconnected way on a global basis, both internally and externally.

Global Geography and Politics

The phenomenon of globalization is complex. There is not complete agreement on the policies that underlie such elements of globalization as tariff agreements, military commitments, and nation-building efforts. Still, globalization is a growing trend, and its importance is likely to expand. Joseph Stiglitz, the former chair of the Council of Economic Advisers, views globalization as follows:

> It would be unfortunate if there was a backlash against globalization because we did not make globalization work for more individuals. It would be unfortunate both for . . . the developed and developing countries. Standard economic theory emphasizes that opening up markets provides opportunities for each country to take advantage of its comparative advantage and provides enhanced scope for efficiency gains from economies of scale. But there is an even more compelling argument for globalization—the encounters between different cultures, the new opportunities which globalization brings, as well as the enhanced competition that accompanies globalization all mean that it can be a tremendous spur for innovation and creativity.[6]

In almost all departments and agencies, presidential appointees confront issues ranging from immigration to genetically modified foods to oil prices. To effectively confront these issues, the appointee must remain current on global political and economic trends regarding these subjects. There are many ways to do this, but the use of the websites of newspapers and other media outlets can be particularly effective. Further, you can use the White House website and also the websites of agencies like the Commerce Department and the State Department as sources of information on global trends. The intelligence community, for example, has created an enhanced capacity to collect and process global information:

> Open-source information (OSINT) is derived from newspapers, journals, radio and television, and the Internet. Intelligence analysts have long used such information to supplement classified data, but systematically collecting open-source information has not been a priority of the U.S. intelligence community. In recent years, given changes in the international environment, there have been calls, from Congress and the 9/11 Commission among others, for a more intense and focused investment in open-source collection and analysis. . . .
>
> A consensus now exists that OSINT must be systematically collected and should constitute an essential component of analytical products. . . . Responding to legislative direction, the intelligence community has . . . created the National Open Source Center. The goal is to perform specialized OSINT acquisition and analysis functions and create a center of excellence that will support and encourage all intelligence agencies.[7]

Global Networks

In *The* Next *Government of the United States,* Don Kettl writes that the complex problems we face today require a focus on solutions rather than structures. "If government's service system resembles a web more than a hierarchy, who is responsible for what? If the government is part of a broader network, is government just one player among many, one claimant at a table with multiple claims on all sides? Who steers the network—if, in fact, the network is being steered? Who safeguards the public interest—and how can it best be done?"[8]

The Defense Department is a leader in using networks to enhance the capacity of the fighter on the battlefield as well as tactical and strategic elements of the command structure. The department has formalized the use of networks into what they refer to as a net-centric environment, which it defines as "a framework for full human and technical connectivity and interoperability that allows all DOD users and mission partners to share the information they need, when they need it, in a form they can understand and act on with confidence, and protects information from those who should not have it."[9] It is not just about the battlefield but also describes "how the future Joint Force will function in that environment across the full range of military operations." The three lessons in this definition are that

—Networks are essential for dealing with complicated missions.

—Networks operate to achieve either broad or narrow purposes, depending on their scope.

—The future will require more and better networks.

Part of your job as a presidential appointee is to use networks across global boundaries to fulfill the president's goals and your agency's mission.

PART II

The Federal Government

This part of the handbook can be considered a road map of the federal government, one that will help you as a presidential appointee find your way forward. It begins with a chapter giving the core principles found in the U.S. Constitution, the very bedrock of the laws of the land. The following chapter gives an overview of the legislative branch, especially the committee system and the legislative processes that you will deal with on a regular basis. The final chapter provides a look at the modern executive branch, the one you will be most involved with.

You will undoubtedly find that government service as an appointee means balancing the day-to-day struggles and compromises with a broader interest in serving the public. It is important to master the processes, but it is similarly important to occasionally take time out and consider the first principles that motivated the American founding. Read the following chapters as you begin your service, and use them as a reference whenever you feel lost or when routine frustrations hamper your ability to serve.

Today's federal government functions in a complex and at times befuddling way. It is unlikely that any one person would have designed the system to work exactly as it does now. The policymaking and government management processes that exist today came about in an organic manner that accommodated innumerable traditions, dilemmas, egos, and practical considerations along the way. Never underestimate the power of experience, and consider the methods and habits of colleagues who are adept at getting things done. These chapters are a roadmap, but the streets of Washington are littered with potholes.

SEVEN

Summary of the U.S. Constitution

The United States Constitution is one of history's great documents. It serves today as a model for governments around the world, though its original passage came only after rigorous debate and compromise. Thomas Jefferson famously called it "the result of the collected wisdom of our country." The men who wrote and signed it at the 1787 Constitutional Convention—lawyers, merchants, farmers—were students of the Renaissance, the Reformation, and the Enlightenment who learned about the social compact from John Locke and Jean-Jacques Rousseau and wove those principles into the American experiment. Henry Clay, the nineteenth-century American statesman who represented Kentucky in both the House of Representatives and the Senate, said that "the Constitution of the United States was made . . . for posterity." At its core, the Constitution does two things: it establishes the United States government, and it reminds the government that there are limits to its power.

All federal employees ultimately derive their power and responsibilities from the Constitution. As a new presidential appointee, you are now both a subject and a trustee of the document.[1] The summary of various key provisions of the Constitution is intended as a compact reference. The entire Constitution can be read at the website of the National Constitution Center.[2] Additional material about the Constitution is also available there.

The Seven Articles

Article I creates the legislative branch, outlining the House of Representatives and the Senate. It sets the term lengths for representatives and senators, establishes minimum age requirements (twenty-five for the House, thirty for the Senate), names the vice president as president of the Senate, and creates the formula for determining each state's representation in the House. It gives the legislative branch the power of impeachment, proscribes compensation for elected officials, and references logistical matters like the keeping of a journal for the public record and mandatory assembly at least once a year. Section 7 authorizes Congress to override a president's veto with a two-thirds majority.

Section 8 of Article I contains all the things the legislative branch is empowered to do. These include the power to collect taxes, impose tariffs, borrow money, regulate commerce, write bankruptcy law, coin money, build post offices, establish federal courts, declare war, raise and support armies, provide and maintain a navy, and make all other laws deemed "necessary and proper" for executing the other powers.

Sections 9 and 10 make explicit what Congress *cannot* do. These clauses were designed to prevent the American government from engaging in the kinds of tactics the Founders found most repugnant about the era's monarchies. Section 9 bans titles of nobility, disallows the suspension of habeas corpus, and prohibits ex post facto laws. It also seeks to settle the interstate conflicts that existed under the Articles of Confederation by prohibiting duties on trade between states. Section 10 similarly bans states from making alliances or declaring war; it notes that the Section 9 limits on the federal government also apply to state governments.

Parts of Article I have been changed. The odious Three-Fifths Compromise, by which slaves were counted as three-fifths of a person for the purposes of calculating a state's representation in the House, was of course rendered obsolete by the Thirteenth Amendment. The Seventeenth Amendment provided for the direct election of senators, replacing the Article I dictum that senators be selected by the state legislatures.

Article II concerns the executive branch. It begins by explaining the Electoral College and setting the eligibility requirements for becoming president (thirty-five years of age and a natural-born citizen). Section 1 of the article also references the line of succession and the oath of office.

Section 2 expounds on the president's powers: serves as the commander in chief of the army and navy, issues pardons as he or she so chooses, and holds the power to appoint ambassadors, judges, and other officials with the advice and consent of the Senate. The president also has the veto power, as referenced in Article I. The remaining sections involve the president's responsibility to inform Congress through State of the Union addresses and Congress's right to impeach for treason, bribery, or other "high crimes and misdemeanors."

Article III provides for the judicial branch, placing its power in the hands of a Supreme Court and other lower courts for Congress to create. It outlines the judicial power held by federal courts: only cases involving citizens versus a state, two citizens of different states, cases involving ambassadors, and other circumstances that would preclude state courts from holding jurisdiction. Section 3 defines treason and mandates either a confession by the accused or at least two witnesses to attest to any treasonous act.

Article IV settles the remaining issues of the states. It contains the "full faith and credit" clause, meaning that any state in the union must honor the laws of any other state. A state may not provide refuge to citizens seeking asylum after breaking the law elsewhere. Section 3 explains the process for admitting new states into the union, and Section 4 mandates that all states establish constitutional republican government.

Article V lays out the procedure for amending the Constitution, which is two-thirds majorities in both houses of Congress, followed by ratification of three-quarters of the states.

Article VI ties up some loose strings: it ensures that the new country will assume all the debt for the money borrowed under the Articles of Confederation, that laws passed by the federal government cannot be ignored by the states and their courts, and that all elected officials and judges must take an oath of office.

Article VII mandates ratification from nine state conventions before the Constitution takes effect, and the signers' names follow.

The First Ten Amendments

The Constitution was eventually ratified, but antifederalists felt the document did not go far enough in securing individual rights. They successfully lobbied for the inclusion of a Bill of Rights during the First Congress in 1789; these ten amendments were ratified by the states in 1791.[3]

—First Amendment: Congress shall make no law respecting an establishment of religion, or prohibiting the free exercise thereof; or abridging the freedom of speech, or of the press; or the right of the people peaceably to assemble, and to petition the government for a redress of grievances.

—Second Amendment: A well-regulated militia, being necessary to the security of a free state, the right of the people to keep and bear arms, shall not be infringed.

—Third Amendment: No soldier shall, in time of peace be quartered in any house, without the consent of the owner, nor in time of war, but in a manner to be prescribed by law.

—Fourth Amendment: The right of the people to be secure in their persons, houses, papers, and effects, against unreasonable searches and seizures, shall not be violated, and no warrants shall issue, but upon probable cause, supported by oath or affirmation, and particularly describing the place to be searched, and the persons or things to be seized.

—Fifth Amendment: No person shall be held to answer for a capital, or otherwise infamous crime, unless on a presentment or indictment of a grand jury, except in cases arising in the land or naval forces, or in the militia, when in actual service in time of war or public danger; nor shall any person be subject for the same offence to be twice put in jeopardy of life or limb; nor shall be compelled in any criminal case to be a witness against himself, nor be deprived of life, liberty, or property, without due process of law; nor shall private property be taken for public use, without just compensation.

—Sixth Amendment: In all criminal prosecutions, the accused shall enjoy the right to a speedy and public trial, by an impartial jury of the state and district wherein the crime shall have been committed, which district shall have been previously ascertained by law, and to be informed of the nature and cause of the accusation; to be confronted with the witnesses against him; to have compulsory process for obtaining witnesses in his favor, and to have the assistance of counsel for his defense.

—Seventh Amendment: In suits at common law, where the value in controversy shall exceed twenty dollars, the right of trial by jury shall be preserved, and no fact tried by a jury, shall be otherwise reexamined in any court of the United States, than according to the rules of the common law.

—Eighth Amendment: Excessive bail shall not be required, nor excessive fines imposed, nor cruel and unusual punishments inflicted.

—Ninth Amendment: The enumeration in the Constitution, of certain rights, shall not be construed to deny or disparage others retained by the people.

—Tenth Amendment: The powers not delegated to the United States by the Constitution, nor prohibited by it to the states, are reserved to the states respectively, or to the people.

Later Amendments

Seventeen new amendments have been ratified since the Bill of Rights. The right to vote was extended to all citizens eighteen years old and older through the Fifteenth, Nineteenth, and Twenty-Sixth Amendments. The Thirteenth Amendment bans slavery, the Sixteenth Amendment allows for an income tax, and the Twenty-Second Amendment limits the president to two terms.

EIGHT

The Legislative Branch

From time to time presidential appointees will be involved in the legislative process, so it is helpful to understand how Congress functions in considering and enacting legislation and how its committee system works.

Enacting Legislation

Legislation can be introduced in either the House or the Senate, except for tax bills, which must come from the House. After a bill is proposed by a member it is referred to the appropriate committee, which will hold hearings if necessary and eventually mark up the bill (see figure 8-1).[1] Marking up is essentially an editing process, by which members can suggest changes to the bill's text before its consideration on the floor. Before it can be brought to the floor, the bill is voted on in committee. If the bill wins the vote of a majority of committee members, it will be put before the full House or Senate according to a schedule determined by House or Senate leadership.

There is a way around the committee process in the House: the discharge petition. If a majority of representatives (218 of the 435) sign a petition demanding a vote on a given piece of legislation, that bill will get a floor vote. One high-profile discharge petition was the 2002 campaign finance reform bill (Shays-Meehan, in the House), which lacked the support of the House Republican leadership but was supported by a majority of members.[2]

F I G U R E   8 - 1 .   How a Bill Becomes a Law

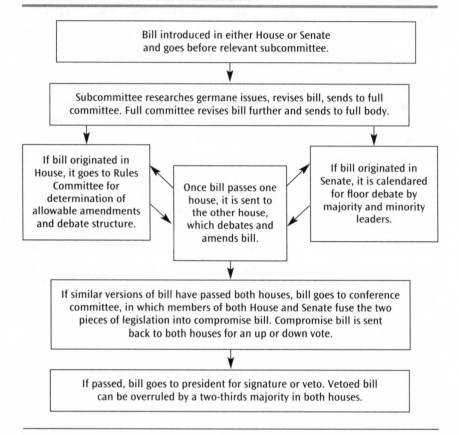

Floor debate is managed much differently in the House than in the Senate. The House has over four times the membership of the Senate and requires more active leadership to manage the legislative process. Debate and voting is tightly regulated by the House Rules Committee, which can control the time spent on any bill and limit the number of amendments under consideration.

In the Senate, any senator can introduce a bill, and the amendment process is much looser than in the House. A single senator (or a group of senators) can filibuster a bill, holding the floor indefinitely to keep a bill from coming to a vote. South Carolina senator Strom Thurmond held the floor for more than twenty-four straight hours to filibuster the 1957 Civil Rights Act. A filibuster can be broken only with a three-fifths vote (sixty senators) to invoke cloture, thus cutting off debate. There is a tradition of senators stalling action when a bill they do not like comes to the floor. The upper body was in some sense designed this way; the Founders certainly intended for it to be more difficult to get a bill through the Senate than through the House. Washington famously told Jefferson that the Senate should cool (or reflect on and moderate) what comes from the House, much as milk was used to cool hot tea.

Once a bill is passed, it goes to the other body for consideration, and the process is repeated. Oftentimes a somewhat different form of a bill will pass each house, compelling a conference committee to consolidate the two bills into one. Conference committees are a crucial, but often under-appreciated, component of the legislative process. They have no pre-scribed reconciliation procedure, so the membership of a conference committee—including its ideological makeup—can have a significant impact on the ultimate legislation. Conference committees typically include the chairs and ranking members of both the House and Senate committees, which is just one of many reasons that the personalities and priorities of committee leaders are so important.

After the conference completes its work, the resulting report is sent back to the House and the Senate for an up or down vote. Another option in the House is to vote to recommit: that is, send the bill back to com-mittee; this happens if the House is dissatisfied with the conference report. A bill that passes both houses is sent to the president for a signature or a veto (either a direct veto or an indirect—pocket—veto). A direct veto can send the bill back to the House and Senate, where a two-thirds majority in each house can override the veto and turn the legislation into law.[3]

Where did all these procedures come from? The basic rules—the majori-ties necessary for passage and veto override—come from the Constitution. But the other rules are most often a product of their times, designed by the congressional leadership to drive the legislative process in a reasonably effi-cient way without sacrificing public input and collaboration. The House's current size would make implementing Senate procedures in the lower body impractical. There was, in fact, a time when the House allowed fili-busters, but it then had around a hundred members.

But the rules change, as do their execution and interpretation. The number of filibusters in the Senate ebbs and flows, depending on the level of contention between the parties, the size of the majorities, and the issues on the table. Recently the Democratic Congress changed a procedural regulation known as Rule 28, intending to make it more difficult for conference committees to insert earmarks into bills during reconciliation.[4] The change has had a mixed effect, making some of the conference committees' routine business tougher to carry out, but it is illustrative of the ever-evolving legislative process that drives the federal government.

The Committee System

The committee system, the core of Congress, is the way bills are evaluated and edited before they go to the floor. Flashy hearings that get a great deal of press coverage, such as the testimony of a Supreme Court nominee or hearings on the impeachment of a president, are the exception rather than the rule. Most committee meetings are staid affairs that get little attention; ideally, representatives and senators use their time to explore an issue's technical questions and to inform their responses.

There are roughly 200 committees, subcommittees, and joint committees in the House of Representatives and the Senate (a significant consolidation took place in 1946, when the number of committees was cut by more than half). The congressional committees are shown in tables 8-1, 8-2, and 8-3, along with their current chairs and ranking members.

From time to time, presidential appointees may be called to testify before one of these committees. In part 1 of this volume, the chapter on leading others contains some advice about testifying before a congressional committee. In general, keep it simple and be respectful. If you do not know the answer to a question, indicate that you will get the information and get back to the committee. This should be done promptly. Committee staffers are typically professionals who have significant service on the committee and are familiar with the issues. Having a good working relationship with staffers will smooth the way for your testimony. Following testimony, you will be given an opportunity to review the record and clarify your remarks, This is not a place for new information but rather a chance to ensure that the record accurately reflects what you intended to say.

TABLE 8-1. **Committees of the U.S. House of Representatives, 110th Congress**

Committee	Chair	Ranking member
Agriculture	Collin Peterson (D-Minn.)	Bob Goodlatte (R-Va.)
Appropriations	David Obey (D-Wisc.)	Jerry Lewis (R-Calif.)
Armed Services	Ike Skelton (D-Mo.)	Duncan Hunter (R-Calif.)
Budget	John Spratt Jr. (D-S.C.)	Paul Ryan (R-Wisc.)
Education and Labor	George Miller (D-Calif.)	Howard McKeon (R-Calif.)
Energy and Commerce	John Dingell (D-Mich.)	Joe Barton (R-Tex.)
Financial Services	Barney Frank (D-Mass.)	Spencer Bachus (R-Ala.)
Foreign Affairs	Howard Berman (D-Calif.)	Ileana Ros-Lehtinen (R-Fla.)
Homeland Security	Bennie Thompson (D-Miss.)	Peter King (R-N.Y.)
House Administration	Robert Brady (D-Pa.)	Vernon Ehlers (R-Mich.)
Judiciary	John Conyers (D-Mich.)	Lamar Smith (R-Tex.)
Natural Resources	Nick Rahall II (D-W.Va.)	Don Young (R-Alaska)
Oversight and Government Reform	Henry Waxman (D-Calif.)	Tom Davis (R-Va.)
Rules	Louise Slaughter (D-N.Y.)	David Dreier (R-Calif.)
Science and Technology	Bart Gordon (D-Tenn.)	Ralph Hall (R-Tex.)
Small Business	Nydia Velaquez (D-N.Y.)	Steve Chabot (R-Ohio)
Standards of Official Conduct	Gene Green (D-Tex.)	Doc Hastings (R-Wash.)
Transportation and Infrastructure	James Oberstar (D-Minn.)	John Mica (R-Fla.)
Veterans' Affairs	Bob Filner (D-Calif.)	Steve Buyer (R-Ind.)
Ways and Means	Charlie Rangel (D-N.Y.)	Jim McCrery (R-La.)
Permanent Select Committee on Intelligence	Silvestre Reyes (D-Tex.)	Peter Hoekstra (R-Mich.)
Select Committee on Energy Independence and Global Warming	Ed Markey (D-Mass.)	James Sensenbrenner (R-Wisc.)

The Powerful Committees

The power to decide on the distribution of federal resources is prized by members in both the House and Senate. As a result, the most sought-after committee assignment is generally Appropriations. The chairs of the appropriations subcommittees are extremely powerful individuals. The Finance Committee in the Senate and the Ways and Means Committee in the House work on tax law and other means of raising revenues, a vital function of government that makes those committees major power centers. All tax bills start in the House Ways and Means Committee.

T A B L E 8 - 2 . Committees of the U.S. Senate, 110th Congress

Committee	Chair	Ranking member
Agriculture, Nutrition, and Forestry	Tom Harkin (D-Iowa)	Saxby Chambliss (R-Ga.)
Appropriations	Robert Byrd (D-W.Va.)	Thad Cochran (R-Miss.)
Armed Services	Carl Levin (D-Mich.)	John McCain (R-Ariz.)
Banking, Housing, and Urban Affairs	Christopher Dodd (D-Conn.)	Richard Shelby (R-Ala.)
Budget	Kent Conrad (D-N.Dak.)	Judd Gregg (R-N.H.)
Commerce, Science, and Transportation	Daniel Inouye (D-Hawaii)	Kay Bailey Hutchison (R-Tex.)
Energy and Natural Resources	Jeff Bingaman (D-N.M.)	Pete Domenici (R-N.M.)
Environment and Public Works	Barbara Boxer (D-Calif.)	James Inhofe (R-Okla.)
Finance	Max Baucus (D-Mont.)	Charles Grassley (R-Iowa)
Foreign Relations	Joseph Biden (D-Del.)	Richard Lugar (R-Ind.)
Health, Education, Labor, and Pensions	Edward Kennedy (D-Mass.)	Michael Enzi (R-Wyo.)
Homeland Security and Governmental Affairs	Joseph Lieberman (I-Conn.)	Susan Collins (R-Maine)
Judiciary	Patrick Leahy (D-Vt.)	Arlen Specter (R-Pa.)
Rules and Administration	Dianne Feinstein (D-Calif.)	Bob Bennett (R-Utah)
Small Business and Entrepreneurship	John Kerry (D-Mass.)	Olympia Snowe (R-Maine)
Veterans' Affairs	Daniel Akaka (D-Hawaii)	Richard Burr (R-N.C.)
Indian Affairs	Byron Dorgan (D-N.Dak.)	Lisa Murkowski (R-Alaska)
Select Committee on Ethics	Barbara Boxer (D-Calif.)	John Cornyn (R-Tex.)
Select Committee on Intelligence	John D. Rockefeller IV (D-W.Va.)	Christopher Bond (R-Mo.)
Special Committee on Aging	Herb Kohl (D-Wisc.)	Gordon Smith (R-Ore.)

As a presidential appointee, you should keep your eye on the workings of the Committee on Oversight and Governmental Reform in the House and the Committee on Homeland Security and Governmental Affairs in the Senate. These are the committees that provide oversight across the executive branch. In addition, your department will have its own authorizing committee, which has substantive power to alter underlying legislation regarding your agency. Authorizing committees also authorize overall levels of spending, subject to final appropriation by the Appropriations Committee. The relationship between the authorizing committee

TABLE 8-3. Joint Committees of the 110th U.S. Congress

Committee	Chair	Vice chair
Joint Committee on Printing	Rep. Robert Brady (D-Pa.)	Sen. Dianne Feinstein (D-Calif.)
Joint Committee on Taxation	Sen. Max Baucus (D-Mont.)	Rep. Charles Rangel (D-N.Y.)
Joint Committee on the Library	Sen. Dianne Feinstein (D-Calif.)	Rep. Robert Brady (D-Pa.)
Joint Economic Committee	Sen. Charles Schumer (D-N.Y.)	Rep. Carolyn B. Maloney (R-N.Y.)

and the Appropriations Committee on budget matters is often contentious, with Appropriations serving as the ultimate arbiter.

All committees have subpoena power, and when the party of the president differs from the majority party in Congress, you can count on committee chairs to use that power aggressively.[5]

Congressional Budget Process

Although the executive branch typically meets the budget timetable, this is not necessarily true for Congress, whose budget resolutions and reconciliation bills are often late, sometimes lagging behind the start of the fiscal year. This can lead to a continuing resolution or a government shutdown and thus be a complicating factor for your agency. In addition, multiple appropriations committees may consider aspects of your agency's budget, which requires you to exercise a special sensitivity to formatting and data requests as well as multiple testimonies on the budget. You should work with your agency budget office to develop an agency-specific budget process that is responsive to the congressional process. It is important to remember that performance information, as well as financial information, should be contained in budget requests and that this information should be consistent with your agency's strategic plans, performance plans, and performance reports. An excellent summary of the process is contained in "The Congressional Budget Process: A Brief Overview," by James Saturno of the Congressional Research Service.

The Government Accountability Office

The mission of the Government Accountability Office (GAO) is to support Congress in meeting its constitutional responsibilities and to help

BOX 8-1. The Evolution of the GAO's High-Risk List

J. Christopher Mihm, U.S. Government Accountability Office

Historically, high-risk areas have been so designated because of traditional vulnerabilities related to fraud, waste, abuse, and mismanagement. In recent years GAO's high-risk program has increasingly focused on those major programs and operations that need urgent attention and transformation in order to ensure that our national government functions in the most economical, efficient, and effective manner possible. Over the past eight years, the GAO has worked to broaden and make much more strategic its high-risk program and has increasingly used the high-risk designation to draw attention to areas associated with needed broad-based transformations. For example, the three high-risk areas added with the last update in January 2007—ensuring the effective protection of technologies critical to the U.S. national security interests, transforming federal oversight of food safety, and financing the nation's transportation system—are all examples of this broader strategic orientation to high risk.

Recent administrations of both parties have focused heavily on areas in GAO's high-risk program, many of which will require both executive branch and congressional actions to achieve needed progress. In fact, this [G. W. Bush] administration has looked to GAO's program in shaping government-wide initiatives such as the President's Management Agenda; over the past several years it has undertaken a focused effort to encourage agencies to develop corrective action plans for high-risk areas. Efforts such as these have made a difference as eighteen areas have been removed from the high-risk list and more than $100 billion in financial benefits have been documented related to our work in the these areas. These results demonstrate that the sustained attention and commitment by Congress and agencies to resolve serious, long-standing, high-risk problems have paid off, as root causes of the government's exposure for more than half of our original high-risk list have been successfully addressed. It will be important for top-level officials in future administrations to continue this emphasis.

improve the performance and ensure the accountability of the federal government for the benefit of the American people. The GAO is an arm of Congress and applies "oversight, insight, and foresight" on its behalf. Every two years the GAO issues its high-risk list. The evolution of this list is presented in box 8-1.

NINE

The Executive Branch

ormal guidance for the conduct of presidential appointees and of their work can be found in various sources, including the Code of Ethics for U.S. Government Service and Presidential Executive Orders and Directives. A well-informed appointee will also be thoroughly familiar with the budget process—its preparation, submission, defense, and execution—and will have a working knowledge of the *Financial Report of the United States Government*.

The Code of Ethics

According to the U.S. Office of Government Ethics, the following standards of ethical conduct for employees of the executive branch are to ensure that every citizen can have complete confidence in the integrity of the federal government.[1]

—Employees shall not hold financial interests that conflict with the conscientious performance of duty.

—Employees shall not engage in financial transactions using nonpublic government information or allow the improper use of such information to further any private interest.

—An employee shall not . . . solicit or accept any gift or other item of monetary value from any person or entity seeking official action from, doing business with, or conducting activities regulated by the employee's agency, or whose interests may be substantially affected by the performance or nonperformance of the employee's duties.

—Employees shall put forth honest effort in the performance of their duties.

—Employees shall not knowingly make unauthorized commitments or promises of any kind purporting to bind the government.

—Employees shall not use public office for private gain.

—Employees shall act impartially and not give preferential treatment to any private organization or individual.

—Employees shall protect and conserve federal property and shall not use it for other than authorized activities.

—Employees shall not engage in outside employment or activities, including seeking or negotiating for employment, that conflict with official government duties and responsibilities.

—Employees shall disclose waste, fraud, abuse, and corruption to appropriate authorities.

—Employees shall satisfy in good faith their obligations as citizens, including all just financial obligations, especially those—such as federal, state, or local taxes—that are imposed by law.

—Employees shall adhere to all laws and regulations that provide equal opportunity for all Americans regardless of race, color, religion, sex, national origin, age, or handicap.

—Employees shall endeavor to avoid any actions creating the appearance that they are violating the law or the ethical standards set forth here. Whether particular circumstances create an appearance that the law or these standards have been violated shall be determined from the perspective of a reasonable person with knowledge of the relevant facts.

Executive Orders and Directives

Executive orders have been used by presidents since the founding of the United States in order to communicate the president's policy preferences to his appointees, Congress, and the public and to guide agency heads. From 1907 until the Federal Register Act of 1936, every executive order was assigned a number by the Department of State. Since 1936 executive orders have been published in the Federal Register, and since 1938 they have been compiled annually in title 3 of the Code of Federal Regulations. Since 1941 they have been published in the *U.S. Code, Congressional and Administrative News* and, since 1965, can also be found in the *Weekly Compilation of Presidential Documents.*

Robert Bedell, a former director of the Office of Federal Procurement Policy and acting general counsel of the Office of Management and Budget, in his testimony before the House Committee on Rules' Subcommittee on Legislative and Budget Process, points out that executive orders are primarily focused on those declarations of the president that have general applicability and legal effect.[2] If a declaration applies only to federal agencies or employees, it is not generally treated as an executive order formally published in the Federal Register.

Bedell lists four critical features of an executive order:

—Coordination of proposed executive orders by the Office of Management and Budget.

—Circulation of proposed executive orders by the general counsel of OMB to interested departments and agencies and concerned parts of the White House staff. If there is a policy disagreement about the wisdom or terms of an executive order, OMB determines or designs an interagency dispute resolution process to address the issues.

—Transmission of the proposed executive order from the director of OMB to the president through the Office of Legal Counsel of the Department of Justice. The Office of Legal Counsel, on behalf of the attorney general, issues an opinion on each proposed order expressing its views whether the proposal is acceptable for form and legality.

—Circulation of the proposed executive order among the White House staff after its receipt from the Department of Justice, to make certain that its terms are acceptable to the president and that there are no further policy issues that need to be resolved.

OMB circulars, memoranda, and bulletins also carry the weight of the executive branch. Generally speaking, circulars are issued by the director of OMB and have an expected life before revision of at least two years. Circulars are often published in draft form, receive extensive comments, and are revised based on these comments. This is especially true for those that affect outside entities.[3]

OMB memoranda can be issued by various officials at OMB, including the heads of such statutory offices as the Office of Federal Financial Management, the Office of Information and Regulatory Affairs, and the Office of Federal Procurement Policy. Memoranda are more likely to be directed to internal purposes of the government, including communicating with agencies or meeting external congressional reporting requirements. OMB bulletins are more immediate in nature and are typically directed to the heads of executive departments and agencies from the director of OMB. There is no clear line of distinction between a bulletin and a memorandum.

In the area of national security, there is a long history since the creation of the National Security Council in 1947 of issuing presidential directives under various names. These include memoranda, review directives, and decision directives.[4]

The Budget Process

As a presidential appointee you will be most involved in the first part of the budget process: the development and execution of the president's budget as it affects your agency. The second part of the budget process is the congressional approval process, which you may be called upon to participate in as well but which is most often managed by the Office of Management and Budget on behalf of the president.

The budget schedule described here was assembled by the Congressional Research Service and is consistent with the overall policy of previous presidents. Three processes happen roughly simultaneously each year, the one that looks backward, the one that looks at the present, and the one that looks forward:

—Calendar year before the fiscal year begins: Budget submissions are developed *during* this year. This process has the longest lead time for the appointee. Detailed information on how the process will evolve and what is involved is contained in various memoranda and circulars from OMB. Central among them is OMB Circular A-11, which contains both general information about the budget process and detailed information about forms and submissions. Appointees would do well to ask their agencies' budget office to explain Circular A-11, particularly in regard to timing and expectations.

—Calendar year in which the fiscal year begins: The new administration will need to work quickly to prepare a budget by the first Monday in February, one that reflects the new president's priorities. Agency involvement in the preparation of the budget will be limited by the practicalities of the need for rapid development of the proposals.

—Calendar years in which fiscal year begins and ends: At the same time that the president's budget is being developed and considered for the next fiscal year, the budget for the current fiscal year is being executed. For the first year, appointees will be executing a budget developed by the prior administration and approved by Congress before the new administration takes office.[5] While it is possible to amend or supplement this budget, in most cases the following fiscal year's budget will be the first one that the appointee will focus on.

The Financial Report

No one expects each presidential appointee to be completely conversant with the annual *Financial Report of the United States Government*. However, knowing the broad elements of what it contains and drawing meaning from these contents is the responsibly of all appointees.

The *Financial Report* was first required by the Government Management Reform Act of 1994; the initial one was produced for fiscal year 1996. The United States Treasury has responsibility for producing the *Financial Report;* it is audited by the Government Accountability Office.

The accounting principles of the *Financial Report* are unique to the federal government. They were developed by and are maintained by the Federal Accounting Standards Advisory Board. One cannot directly compare these accounting principles to those of the private sector or even other governments because of unique legislative and regulatory requirements. While the Advisory Board develops and maintains the accounting principles, they are promulgated for the executive branch by the secretary of the Treasury and the director of the Office of Management and Budget. An understanding of financial concepts such as "on budget," "off budget," "trust funds," and "debt held by the public" is important to understanding the finances of the federal government.[6]

The *Financial Report* does not typically make projections about the future, but the "Citizens Guide" to the report for 2007 (developed by the U.S. Treasury) has some interesting observations on the "unsustainable" nature of the federal government's financial position. The GAO and the National Academy of Public Administration have also done work in this area. For the appointee, the resolution of the dilemma posed by an unsustainable fiscal future is likely to be key to the priorities of the next administration and those that follow.

The Government Accountability Office states the following in its audit report for fiscal 2007:

> While significant progress has been made in improving financial management since the U.S. government began preparing consolidated financial statements 11 years ago, three major impediments continue to prevent us from rendering an opinion on the accrual basis consolidated financial statements: (1) serious financial management problems at the Department of Defense, (2) the federal government's inability to adequately account for and reconcile intra-governmental activity and balances between federal agencies, and (3) the federal government's ineffective process for preparing the consolidated financial statements. Until the problems outlined in our audit report are adequately addressed, they will continue to have adverse implications for the federal government and American taxpayers.[7]

This form of opinion is referred to as a disclaimer. It means that the GAO is unable to rely on the data collected and reported by federal agencies to fairly render an opinion on the financial condition of the federal government as a whole. Until the problems noted above are remedied, it is unlikely that the federal government as a whole will get an unqualified audit opinion.

The Chief Financial Officers Act of 1990 and the Government Management Reform Act of 1994, along with legislation creating agencies such as the Department of Homeland Security, have all required the creation and auditing of individual agency financial statements. These financial statements are audited either by the GAO, each agency's inspector general, or outside accounting firms working with the agency's inspector general. An agency can receive one of three opinions on their financial statements: unqualified (or clean), qualified, or disclaimed.[8]

The "Citizens Guide" in the *2007 Financial Report of the United States Government* also shows that the cost of running the government exceeded the revenues of the government by $275.5 billion dollars in fiscal year 2007, increasing the gross debt of the federal government to $9.8 trillion. In addition, current social insurance programs (primarily Social Security and Medicare and other federal liabilities) create an additional exposure, in present-value terms over the next seventy-five years, of between $40 trillion and $45 trillion under current assumptions and program structures.

Commenting on these figures in the GAO audit opinion, former comptroller general David Walker focuses on the effect on future generations:

> Considering this projected gap in social insurance, in addition to reported liabilities (e.g., debt held by the public and federal employee and veterans benefits payable) and other implicit commitments and contingencies that the federal government has pledged to support, the federal government's fiscal exposures totaled approximately $53 trillion as of September 30, 2007, up more than $2 trillion from September 30, 2006, and an increase of more than $32 trillion from about $20 trillion as of September 30, 2000. This translates into a current burden of about $175,000 per American, or approximately $455,000 per American household.[9]

Supplemental Reading

As this handbook was being written, several veteran presidential appointees observed that it would be useful to include material about the appointment and confirmation processes. Fortunately, there are three excellent publications on this subject.

The Plum Book

The Government Printing Office describes the Plum Book as follows: "Every four years, just after the presidential election, the *United States Government Policy and Supporting Positions,* commonly known as the

Plum Book, is published, alternately, by the Senate Committee on Governmental Affairs and the House Committee on Government Reform. The Plum Book is used to identify presidentially appointed positions within the federal government."

For those seeking a presidential appointment the Plum Book is like a Christmas catalog of federal job opportunities. It contains the full panoply of executive schedule, senior executive service, foreign service, schedule C, and GS-14-level (and above) positions that are "exempted from competitive civil service by law because of the confidential or policy-determining nature of the position duties."

Key information is supplied about each position: location, title, name of the incumbent, type of appointment, and pay. For appointments with an expiration date, the information includes tenure and term. The information is given for both the legislative and executive branches, the executive branch openings being listed by department, agency, or government corporation.

The Prune Book

For nearly twenty years the Council for Excellence in Government has produced the Prune Book, a guide written specifically to help the incoming administration with one of its most difficult tasks—staffing the sub-cabinet positions that will carry out the new president's agenda. The council lists the management and executive jobs that require that the appointees be prunes; that is, "plums seasoned by wisdom and experience, with a much thicker skin."

For 2009 the council is taking a different publishing approach with a web-based publication it calls Prunes 2.0. Not only will Prunes 2.0 profile jobs, it will also describe the qualifications and attributes that the president and the Senate should look for in appointees for these jobs. The jobs listed in Prunes 2.0 are selected for

—The size and scope of their management duties,

—Their congressional and public visibility,

—The consequences of their failure,

—And their priority level.

By the time this handbook is available to the public, Prunes 2.0 should be online at the council's website.[10]

A Survivor's Guide for Presidential Nominees

The *Survivor's Guide,* published by the Brookings Institution in 2000, is designed to help individuals answer the call of the president by giving an unbiased view of the appointments process.[11] The guide includes information on stages of the appointments process, key gatekeepers, financial disclosure, dealing with the media, and examples of questions asked by Senate committees. The book's appendixes display the forms the nominee will be required to fill out. Many who struggled with the nomination process before publication of the *Survivor's Guide* dearly wish it had been available to them.

Notes

Part One

1. Office of Personnel Management (www.opm.gov/ses/recruitment/ecq.asp).

2. Richard E. Boyatzis, *The Competent Manager: A Model for Effective Performance* (New York: John Wiley and Sons, 1982), p. 21.

3. Mary Ellen Joyce, "Developing 21st Century Public Leaders: Competency-Based Executive Development," Ph.D. dissertation, George Washington University, 2006, p. 60.

4. John W. Gardner, *Self-Renewal: The Individual and the Innovative Society* (New York: W. W. Norton, 1995), pp. 11–12.

5. Joseph A. Califano Jr., *Inside: A Public and Private Life* (New York: Public Affairs, 2004), p. 3.

Chapter One

1. Jim Wolf, "U.S. Auditors Bash Air Force over Refueling Tanker," Reuters, June 18, 2008.

2. Graham Allison, "Public and Private Management: Are They Fundamentally Alike in All Unimportant Respects?" *Proceedings of the Public Management Research Conference* (Washington: Office of Personnel Management, 1979), p. 29.

3. Pew Research Center for the People and the Press, "Federal Government's Favorable Ratings Slump," May 14, 2008.

4. Robert Kaplan and David Norton, *The Balanced Scorecard: Translating Strategy into Action* (Harvard Business School Press, 1996), p. 7.

5. U.S. Office of Personnel Management, "Recruitment and Selection, Executive and Core Qualifications" (www.opm.gov/ses/recruitment/ecq.asp).

6. James Q. Wilson, *Bureaucracy: What Government Agencies Do and Why They Do It* (New York: Basic Books, 1989), p. 158.

7. U.S. Environmental Protection Agency, "2006–2011 EPA Strategic Plan" (www.epa.gov/cfo/plan/plan.htm).

8. Robert Shea, comments, Annual Meeting of the National Academy of Public Administration, November 2007. Performance data for more than a thousand federal programs subjected to PART are given on the website ExpectMore.gov.

9. Robert D. Behn, *Rethinking Democratic Accountability* (Brookings, 2001).

10. See www.theacsi.org.

11. See "IRS Strategic Plan 2005-2009" for a detailed explanation of the IRS approach to performance measurement (www.irs.gov/pub/irs-utl/strategic_plan_05-09.pdf).

12. "ODNI Launches New Website" (www.dni.gov/press_releases/20080506_release.pdf).

13. National Response Framework (www.gao.gov/highlights/d08768high.pdf).

14. David Osborne and Ted Gaebler, *Reinventing Government: How the Entrepreneurial Spirit Is Transforming the Public Sector* (Reading, Mass.: Addison-Wesley, 1992).

15. Mark H. Moore, *Creating Public Value: Strategic Management in Government* (Harvard University Press, 1995), p. 18.

16. Ingrid Bonn, "Developing Strategic Thinking as a Core Competency," *Management Decision* 139, no.1 (2001): 63–71.

17. This and other diagnostic tools are available at the website, www.strategyllp.com.

18. Peter M. Senge, *The Fifth Discipline: The Art and Practice of the Learning Organization* (New York: Doubleday Business, 2008), p. 68.

19. Sveriges Riksbank Prize in Economic Sciences in Memory of Alfred Nobel, 2005, press release.

Chapter Two

1. John P. Kotter, *Leading Change* (Harvard Business School Press, 1996).

2. Henry G. Cisneros, *Defensible Space: Deterring Crime and Building Community* (U.S. Department of Housing and Urban Development, 1995), p. 3.

3. Clay Johnson, memorandum, Office of Management and Budget, September 10, 2007.

4. James MacGregor Burns, *Transforming Leadership: The Pursuit of Happiness* (New York: Atlantic Monthly Press, 2003), p. 167.

5. Edmund Morris, *Theodore Rex* (New York: Random House, 2001), p. 511.

6. John P. Kotter, *What Leaders Really Do* (Harvard Business School Press, 1999), p. 83.

7. See www.whitehouse.gov/omb/budget/fy2002/mgmt.pdf.

8. Ibid.

9. Edgar H. Schein, *Organizational Culture and Leadership* (San Francisco: Jossey-Bass, 1985), pp. 6–7.

10. Quoted in Frances Hesselbein, *Leading for Innovation and Organizing for Results* (San Francisco: Jossey-Bass, 2002), p. 89.

11. Elaine C. Kamarck, "Government Innovation around the World," Working Paper RWP04-010 (Ash Institute for Democratic Governance and Innovation, John F. Kennedy School of Government, 2003).

12. Innovations in American Government Awards (http://ashinstitute.harvard. edu/).

13. Ben R. Rich and Leo Janos, *Skunk Works: A Personal Memoir of My Years at Lockheed* (Boston: Back Bay Books, 1994), p. 6.

14. Franklin D. Roosevelt, *Looking Forward* (New York: John Day, 1933), p. 51.

15. Harvey G. Cox, *On Not Leaving It to the Snake* (New York: Macmillan, 1967), p. viii.

16. Malcolm Gladwell, *Blink: The Power of Thinking without Thinking* (New York: Little, Brown, 2005), pp. 143–44.

17. Dan Caterinicchia, "Exploring Intuitive Decisionmaking," *Federal Computer Week*, December 8, 2002 (www.fcw.com/print/8_49/news/78285-1.html).

18. See thinkexist.com/quotation/a_pessimist_sees_the_difficulty_in_every/15269. html.

19. David Shribman, "Candidates with High Hopes Resonate with American Voters," *Pittsburgh Post Gazette*, May 12, 2007, p. 7.

Chapter Three

1. G. Edward DeSeve, "The Federal Budget: Connecting Resources to Results," *Government Finance Review* 12 (August 1996): 31.

2. Apportionment is defined as "the action by which the Office of Management and Budget (OMB) distributes amounts available for obligation, including budgetary reserves established pursuant to law, in an appropriation or fund account. An apportionment divides amounts available for obligation by specific time periods (usually quarters), activities, projects, objects, or a combination thereof. The amounts so apportioned limit the amount of obligations that may be incurred. An apportionment may be further subdivided by an agency into allotments, suballotments, and allocations. In apportioning any account, some funds may be reserved to provide for contingencies or to effect savings made possible pursuant to the Anti-deficiency Act." *A Glossary of Terms Used in the Federal Budget Process*, GAO-05-734SP (www.gao.gov/new.items/d05734sp.pdf).

3. Association of Government Accountants, *Scoring: Financial Management and Oversight Efforts*, annual CFO survey (Alexandria, Va., 2007).

4. See, for example, OMB Circular A-123 (www.whitehouse.gov/omb/circulars/a123/a123.html).

5. For a more complete discussion, see Partnership for Public Service, "Federal Human Capital: The Perfect Storm" (Washington, 2007).

6. Government Accountability Office, "High-Risk Series: An Update," GAO-07-310, January 2007, p. 39.

7. Government Accountability Office, "Human Capital: Federal Workforce Challenges in the 21st Century," GAO-07-556T, March 6, 2007.

8. Matthew Guthridge and others, "The People Problem in Talent Management," *McKinsey Quarterly*, issue 2 (2006): 6–8.

9. Chief Acquisition Officers Council (www.caoc.gov/), Chief Financial Officers Council (www.cfoc.gov), Chief Human Capital Officers Council (www.chcoc.gov), and Chief Information Officers Council (www.cioc).

10. Steven Kelman, "Remaking Federal Procurement," Working Paper 3 (John F. Kennedy School of Government, 2002), p. 2.

11. See www.fpdsng.com.

12. *Urgent Reform Required: Army Expeditionary Contracting,* Report of the Commission on Army Acquisition and Program Management in Expeditionary Operations, October 2007, p. 3.

13. Here is an example from ancient Greece featuring Aristides the Just: "Pretending now to repent . . . of his former practice, and carrying himself with more remissness, he became acceptable to such as pillaged the treasury by not detecting or calling them to an exact account. So that those who had their fill of the public money began highly to applaud Aristides, and sued to the people making interest to have him once more chosen treasurer. But when they were upon the point of election, he reproved the Athenians. 'When I discharged my office well and faithfully,' said he, 'I was insulted and abused; but now that I have allowed the public thieves in a variety of malpractices, I am considered an admirable patriot. I am more ashamed, therefore, of this present honour than of the former sentence; and I commiserate your condition, with whom it is more praiseworthy to oblige ill men than to conserve the revenue of the public'" (classics.mit.edu/Plutarch/aristide.html).

14. Rep. Henry A. Waxman (D-Calif.), speech to the Professional Services Council, September 10, 2007 (www.house.gov/waxman/pdfs/speech_psc_9-10-2007.pdf).

15. Stan Z. Soloway, president, Professional Services Council, communication with author.

16. Office of Personnel Management, "Recruitment and Selection, Executive and Core Qualifications" (www.opm.gov/ses/recruitment/ecq.asp).

17. See www.innovations.harvard.edu.

18. See www.sans.org.

Chapter Four

1. Patrick J. Montana and Bruce H. Charnov, *Management* (New York: Barron's Business Review Series, 1987), p. 211.

2. James MacGregor Burns, *Transforming Leadership* (New York: Atlantic Monthly Press, 2003); Daniel Goleman and others, *Primal Leadership: Realizing the Power of Emotional Intelligence* (Boston: Harvard Business School Press, 2002); Warren G. Bennis and Burt Nanus, *Leaders: Strategies for Taking Charge* (New York: HarperCollins, 1985)

3. See jepson.richmond.edu.

4. From Presidential Commission from William Jefferson Clinton for G. Edward DeSeve, May 25, 1995.

5. Burns, *Transforming Leadership.*

6. Bennis and Nanus, *Leaders,* p. 31.

7. Goleman and others, *Primal Leadership,* preface.

8. Joel R. DeLuca, *Political Savvy: Systemic Approaches to Leadership Behind the Scenes* (Berwyn, Pa.: Evergreen Business Group, 1999).

9. President Ronald Reagan, Farewell Address, January 11, 1989.

10. Peggy Noonan, *What I Saw at the Revolution: A Political Life in the Reagan Era* (New York: Random House, 2003), p. 68.

11. These are specified in OMB Circular A-19.

12. The Library of Congress is an excellent source of information about the committees. In addition, the website thomas.loc.gov/home/laws_made.html describes the legislative process.

13. A unique resource for government executives is supplied by www.plainlanguage.gov, a website dedicated to improving written communication in the federal government. For a history of the effort over the last thirty-plus years, see www.plainlanguage.gov/whatispl/history/locke.cfm. A particularly effective example of grueling testimony is that of General David Petraeus (www.youtube.com/watch?v=dmb_r5ckzn8).

14. John Dumond and Rick Eden, "Improving Government Process: From Velocity Management to Presidential Appointments," in *High-Performance Government: Structure, Leadership, Incentives,* edited by Robert Klitgard and Paul C. Light (Santa Monica, Calif.: RAND, 2005).

15. Office of the Director of National Intelligence, July 2006.

16. Government Accountability Office, "High Risk Series: An Update," GAO-05-350T, February 2005, p. 32.

17. Graham T. Allison, "Public and Private Management: Are They Fundamentally Alike in All Unimportant Respects?" in *Public Administration: Concepts and Cases,* edited by Jay M. Shafritz, E. W. Russell, and Christopher Borick, 5th ed. (Boston: Houghton Mifflin, 1992), p. 400.

18. Dana Michael Harsell, "Working with Career Executives to Manage for Results" (www.businessofgovernment.org/pdf).

19. H. Brinton Milward and Keith Provan, "The Public Manager's Guide to Network Management," Working Paper 1008-04 (Eller College of Management, University of Arizona, September 2004).

20. Rob Cross and Andrew Parker, *The Hidden Power of Social Networks* (Harvard Business School Press, 2004).

21. Florence Olsen, "The Collaboration Gurus," *Federal Computer Week,* March 3, 2008.

22. See www.napawash.org/collaborationproject.html.

23. For a more detailed discussion of types of networks, see G. Edward DeSeve, "Creating Public Value Using Managed Networks," in *Transforming Public Leadership for the 21st Century,* edited by Ricardo S. Morse and others (Armonk, N.Y.: M. E. Sharpe, 2007).

24. Taylor Branch, *Parting the Waters: America in the King Years, 1954–1963* (New York: Simon and Schuster, 1989), p. 221.

25. Roger Fisher, William Ury, and Bruce Patton, *Getting to Yes: Negotiating Agreement without Giving In* (New York: Penguin, 1991).

26. For a more detailed presentation for practitioners, see Michael L. Moffitt and Robert C. Bordone, *The Handbook of Dispute Resolution* (San Francisco: Jossey-Bass, 2005).

27. For a detailed summary of this program and the individual training sessions, and for an evaluation of the program, see www.wilsoncenter.org.

28. Montana and Charnov, *Management,* p. 211.

29. Rosabeth Moss Kanter, interview, *Management Consulting News* 4, no. 1 (2005) (managementconsultingnews.com).

30. Peter Drucker, "There's More than One Kind of Team," *Wall Street Journal,* February 11, 1992, p. A16.

31. The Center for Creative Leadership is an excellent source for these techniques. See www.ccl.org.

32. H. George Frederickson, *The Spirit of Public Administration* (San Francisco: Jossey-Bass, 1996).

33. H. George Frederickson, "The State of Social Equity in American Public Administration" (Washington: National Academy of Public Administration, February 2005), p. 1.

34. Mark Thompson, "'Don't Ask, Don't Tell' Turns 15," *Time,* January 28, 2008.

35. See www.napawash.org/SEPEquityRosenbloom.pdf.

36. Columbia Accident Investigation Board, August 2003 (caib.nasa.gov/news/report/pdf/vol1/chapters/introduction.pdf).

37. Scott E. Page, *The Difference: How the Power of Diversity Creates Better Groups, Firms, Schools, and Societies* (Princeton University Press, 2007), p. xxiv.

Chapter Five

1. Elmer B. Staats, "Public Service and the Public Interest," *Public Administration Review* 48 (March-April 1988): 601.

2. John Gardner, *Personal Journals* (www.pbs.org/johngardner/sections/writings.html).

3. James L. Perry, "Measuring Public Service Motivation: An Assessment of Construct Reliability and Validity," *Journal of Public Administration Research and Theory* 6 (January 1996): 5–22.

4. See www.opm.gov/ses/competencies.asp.

5. Mark H. Moore *Creating Public Value: Strategic Management in Government* (Harvard University Press, 1995); for the traditional concept, see G. Edward DeSeve, "Creating Public Value Using Managed Networks," in *Transforming Public Leadership for the 21st Century,* edited by Ricardo S. Morse and others (Armonk, N.Y.: M. E. Sharpe, 2007).

6. Government Accountability Office, "Performance and Accountability Report 2007," GAO-08-2SP, p. 2.

7. See www.gao.gov/special.pubs/longterm/wakeuptour.html.

8. National Academy of Public Administration, *Ensuring the Future Prosperity of America: Addressing the Fiscal Future,* November 2005 (www.napawash.org/Pubs/12-5-05FiscalFuture.pdf).

9. Marcus Buckingham and Donald O. Clifton coined this term in their book *Now, Discover Your Strengths* (New York: Free Press, 2001).

10. G. Richard Shell and Mario Moussa, *The Art of Woo* (New York: Portfolio, 2007), p. 17.

11. David Riesman, *The Lonely Crowd* (Yale University Press, 1950).

12. The original developers of the personality inventory were Katharine Cook Briggs and her daughter, Isabel Briggs Myers, who began creating the indicator during World War II. The *Myers-Briggs Type Indicator,* first published in 1962, focuses on normal populations and emphasizes the value of naturally occurring differences.

13. Carol S. Pearson, *Awakening the Heroes Within: Twelve Archetypes to Help Us Find Ourselves and Transform the World* (New York: HarperOne, 1991), p. 3.

14. See www.whitehouse.gov/results/tools/cardtranscript.html.

15. See www.usoge.gov/index.html.

16. See wikipedia.org/wiki/political_scandals_of_the_United_States; and library. syr.edu/research/internet/political_science/prezscandal.html.

17. Warren Bennis and Burt Nanus, *Leaders: Strategies for Taking Charge* (New York: Harper/Collins, 1985), p. 63.

18. Donald F. Kettl, *System under Stress: Homeland Security and American Politics* (Washington: CQ Press, 2004), p. 81.

19. "Recruitment and Selection, Executive and Core Qualifications" (www.opm. gov/ses/recruitment/ecq.asp).

20. Peter M. Senge, *The Fifth Discipline: The Art and Practice of the Learning Organization* (New York: Doubleday/Currency, 2008), p. 14.

21. Stephen Goldsmith and William Eggers, *Unlocking the Power of Networks: Keys to High-Performance Government* (Brookings, 2009).

22. Bennis and Nanus, *Leaders,* p. 41.

23. President Kennedy, remarks at the dedication of the Aerospace Medical Health Center, San Antonio, November 21, 1963.

24. Steve App, former deputy CFO, Department of the Treasury, written communication to author for this publication.

25. Rosabeth Moss Kanter, "How Leaders Gain and Lose Confidence," *Leader to Leader,* no. 35 (Winter 2005): 21.

26. Ibid., p. 24.

27. Stephen R. Covey, *The 7 Habits of Highly Effective People* (New York: Simon and Schuster, 1989), p. 235.

28. Robert B. Reich, *Locked in the Cabinet* (New York: Knopf, 1997), pp. 89, 135–36.

29. Daniel Goleman and others, *Primal Leadership: Realizing the Power of Emotional Intelligence* (Boston: Harvard Business School Press, 2002), p. 3.

30. Ibid., p. 39.

Chapter Six

1. Mary Ellen Joyce, "Developing 21st Century Public Leaders: Competency-Based Executive Development," Ph.D. dissertation, George Washington University, 2006.

2. Donald F. Kettl, *The Next Government of the United States: Challenges for Performance in the 21st Century* (Washington: IBM Center for the Business of Government, 2005), p. 7.

3. Julie Gerberding, Webb lectures (www.mapawash.org). Also see Duncan J. Watts, *Small Worlds: The Dynamics of Networks between Order and Randomness* (Princeton University Press, 1999).

4. "Transcript: A TimesSelect/TimesTalks Event on Globalization," *New York Times,* April 25, 2006 (http://select.nytimes.com/2006/04/25/opinion/25friedman -transcript.html?pagewanted=all).

5. U.S. Department of State, Overseas Presence Advisory Panel, "America's Overseas Presence in the 21st Century," November 1999, p. 7.

6. Joseph Stiglitz, "Globalisation Fails to Help the Poorest," *Times of London,* February 19, 2007, p. 48.

7. Richard A. Best Jr. and Alfred Cumming, "Open Source Intelligence (OSINT): Issues for Congress" (Congressional Research Service, December 5, 2007), quotation in the frontmatter.

8. Kettl, *The* Next *Government of the United States,* p. 9.
9. See www.defenselink.mil/cio-nii/docs/services_strategy.pdf, p. 1.

Chapter Seven

1. Brookings, "The Presidential Appointment Initiative: A Survivor's Guide for Presidential Nominees," November 2000 (www.appointee.brookings.org/), p. 123.
2. See http://constitutioncenter.org.
3. National Archives (www.archives.gov/exhibits/charters/constitution.html).

Chapter Eight

1. In this chapter the term *committees* refers to full committees, their subcommittees, and joint committees.
2. Juliet Eilperin, "Hastert Pledges to Fight Campaign Finance Bill," *Washington Post,* February 7, 2002, p. A1.
3. An explanation of how a bill becomes law is also available at www.senate.gov/reference/resources/pdf/howourlawsaremade.pdf.
4. "Rules of Debate; Tactical Skirmishes Intensified in 110th Congress," *Roll Call,* January 28, 2008.
5. You can find any committee website by navigating the House and Senate websites (www.house.gov; www.senate.gov). An additional resource for information about current bills and committee schedules is the Library of Congress website (thomas.loc.gov).

Chapter Nine

1. See 5 C.F.R. pt. 2635 as amended at 67 FR 61761-61762 (www.usoge.gov/).
2. See rules.house.gov/Archives/rules_bede08.htm.
3. See, for example, OMB Circular A-21, "Cost Principles for Educational Institutions." For a listing of OMB circulars, memoranda, and bulletins from 1995 forward, see www.whitehouse.gov/omb/memoranda/index.html.
4. A summary of these documents along with related executive orders since 1947 can be found at www.fas.org/irp/offdocs/direct.htm.
5. If Congress delays final approval of any appropriations bills until after the 2008 elections, a continuing resolution would allow agencies to operate for a designated period at a level of spending similar to that of the prior year.
6. There are several places to go for information about these terms, including the Government Accountability Office (www.gao.gov); the Congressional Budget Office (www.cbo.gov); and Allen Schick, *The Federal Budget: Politics, Policy, and Process* (Brookings, 1994), esp. the glossary, p. 287.
7. *2007 Financial Report of the United States Government,* p. 34.
8. A list of the audit status of each major agency can be found at www.gao.gov/financial/fy2007/mangmntdis.pdf.
9. Ibid., p. 33.
10. See www.excelgov.org.
11. *A Survivor's Guide for Presidential Nominees* (Brookings, 2000).

Index

Accountability: accountability environment, 7–10; accounting and, 35, 36; balanced scorecard and, 10–12; budgets and, 8, 35; financial reports and, 36; contracting and, 39; management of, 52; measuring results, 10–17; of presidents, 87; in public versus private organizations, 9–10; team building and, 56; trust and, 72. *See also* Government Accountability Office

Accounting, 8, 14, 34, 35, 36, 37, 102

ACE project. *See* Automated Commercial Environment project

Acquisition, 40b. *See also* Contracting; Procurement

ACSI. *See* American Customer Satisfaction Index

Administrations, 2, 3, 52, 105–06

Afghanistan, 39

Agencies: analyses of customer attitudes by, 15; appointees and career employees in, 49–61; authorizing committees of, 95–96; balanced scorecard and, 10–12; budgets and financial management in, 8, 34–35, 95–97, 101–02, 103–04; change in, 21–30; communications of, 78–79; contracting and procurement by, 38–39, 40b; customers of, 15–16; ethics issues of, 68; evaluation of, 9–10; five-star framework and, 18;

high-risk list of, 9, 21, 35; human capital and resources in, 35, 37–38, 49; leadership of, 9; mission and mission execution of, 16; outputs and outcomes of, 12; oversight of, 8–9; performance measures and reports, 13–14, 96; public acceptance and opinion of, 16; strategic planning and, 8, 13, 16, 96; systemic transformation in, 49; trust and, 16; Y2K computer challenge and, 27. *See also* Appointees; Civil service; Government; Leaders and leadership; Managers and management; *individual agencies and departments*

Air Force, 9, 29

Allen, Thad, 70

Allison, Graham, 9–10, 50

Al Qaeda, 78

American Customer Satisfaction Index (ACSI), 15

AmeriCorps programs, 46

Antidiscrimination laws, 57

Appointees: budget issues and, 34–35, 64–65, 96, 101–02; career employees and, 50–51; collaboration and, 51–56; Code of Ethics, 98–99; conflicts of, 2–3, 15, 52, 54–55; Congress and, 95–96; contracting and, 38, 40b; corrective actions by, 41b; equity and, 56–59; goals and